Transforming Work

NEW PERSPECTIVES IN ORGANIZATIONAL LEARNING,
PERFORMANCE, AND CHANGE

JERRY W. GILLEY, SERIES EDITOR

Transforming Work
by Patricia E. Boverie and Michael Kroth

Philosophy and Practice of
Organizational Learning, Performance, and Change
by Jerry W. Gilley, Peter Dean, and Laura Bierema

Assessing the Financial Benefits of
Human Resource Development
by Richard A. Swanson

The Manager as Change Agent
by Jerry W. Gilley, Scott A. Quatro,
Erik Hoekstra, Doug D. Whittle, and Ann Maycunich

Transforming Work

The Five Keys to
Achieving Trust, Commitment, and
Passion in the Workplace

Patricia E. Boverie and Michael Kroth

New Perspectives in Organizational Learning,
Performance, and Change

PERSEUS
PUBLISHING

Many of the designations used by manufacturers and sellers to distinguish their products are claimed as trademarks. Where those designations appear in this book and Perseus Publishing was aware of a trademark claim, the designations have been printed in initial capital letters.

CIP card available from the Library of Congress.

Copyright © 2001 by Patricia E. Boverie and Michael Kroth

Perseus Publishing is a member of the Perseus Books Group.

Find us on the World Wide Web at http://www.perseuspublishing.com

Perseus Publishing books are available at special discounts for bulk purchases in the U.S. by corporations, institutions, and other organizations. For more information, please contact the Special Markets Department at the Perseus Books Group, 11 Cambridge Center, Cambridge, MA 02142, or call (617) 252–5298.

Set in 11-point Minion by Perseus Books Group

First printing, December 2001

1 2 3 4 5 6 7 8 9 10—04 03

We dedicate this book to our fathers, who devoted their lives to the health and the growth of others. They have touched us irrevocably and deeply, and made a true difference in the lives of the thousands of patients and students who were privileged to come into contact with them. Their lives epitomize the transformational power of passionate work.

To my father, Robert "Pete" Boverie, M.D. (1912–1974).

You raised me in love, guided me with patience, and blessed me with life.

To my father, Dr. Roger L. Kroth.

Your passion for learning, your love of teaching, and your care for others have been my inspiration, my aspiration, and the North Star that guides my life.

Permission Acknowledgments

From *The Prophet* by Kahlil Gibran, copyright © 1923 by Kahlil Gibran and renewed 1951 by Administrators C.T.A. of Kahlil Gibran Estate of Mary G. Gibran. Used by permission of Alfred A. Knopf, a division of Random House, Inc.

From *Nuts!* by Kevin Freiberg and Jacquelyn Freiberg, copyright © 1996. Used by permission of Bard Press, Inc.

From *The Heart Aroused* by David Whyte, copyright © 1994 by David Whyte. Used by permission of Doubleday, a division of Random House, Inc.

From *In Search of Excellence* by Thomas J. Peters and Robert Waterman Jr. Copyright © 1982 by Thomas J. Peters and Robert Waterman Jr. Reprinted by permission of HarperCollins Publishers Inc.

From *The Art of Happiness: A Handbook for the Living* by His Holiness the Dalai Lama and Howard C. Cutler. Used by permission of Riverhead Books, a division of Penguin Putnam, Inc.

From *How to Find the Work You Love* by Laurence G. Boldt. Copyright © 1996 by Laurence G. Boldt. Used by permission of Viking Press, a division of Penguin Putnam Inc.

From *Working: People Talking About What They Do All Day and How They Feel About It* by Studs Terkel. Copyright © 1974. Reprinted by permission of the New Press.

From *Built to Last* by James C. Collins and Jerry I. Porras. Copyright © 1994 by James C. Collins and Jerry I. Porras. Reprinted by permission of HarperCollins Publishers, Inc.

From "Workplace Learning and Generation X" by Breda Bova and Michael Kroth. *Journal of Workplace Learning* 13, no. 2, March 2001.

From "Closing the Gap: The Mentoring of Generation X" by Breda Bova and Michael Kroth. *MPAEA Journal of Adult Education,* summer 1999, pp. 7–17.

From *The Triangle of Love: Intimacy, Passion, Commitment* by Dr. Robert Sternberg. Copyright © 1987. Reprinted by permission of Dr. Robert Sternberg.

From "Closing the Gap: The Mentoring of Generation X" by Breda Bova and Michael Kroth. *MPAEA Journal of Adult Education,* summer 1999, pp. 7–17.

From *The Passionate Organization* by James R. Lucas. Reprinted by permission of James R. Lucas, author of *The Passionate Organization* and nine other books, speaker, and president of Luman Consultants International.

From *Learning As Transformation* by Jack Mezirow. Copyright © 2000. Reprinted by permission of Jossey-Bass, Inc., a subsidiary of John Wiley and Sons, Inc.

From *Transitions: Making Sense of Life's Changes* by William Bridges. Copyright © 1980 by William Bridges and Associates, Inc. Reprinted by permission of Perseus Books Publishers, a member of Perseus Books, LLC.

From *Working with Emotional Intelligence* by Daniel Goleman. Copyright © 1998 by Daniel Goleman. Used by permission of Bantam Books, a division of Random House, Inc., and by Brockman Inc. for UK rights.

Excerpts from *On Becoming a Person* by Carl Rogers. Copyright © 1961. Reprinted by permission of Houghton Mifflin Company. All rights reserved.

From *The Adult Learner: A Neglected Species,* 4th ed., by Malcolm Knowles. Copyright © Butterworth Heinemann. Houston, Tex.: Gulf Publishing Company, 1990.

From *Experiential Learning* by Davis Kolb. Copyright © 1984. Reprinted by permission of Pearson Education, Inc., Upper Saddle River, N.J.

Publisher's Note

Organizations are living systems, in a constant state of dynamic evolution. *New Perspectives in Organizational Learning, Performance, and Change* is designed to showcase the most current theory and practice in human resource and organizational development, exploring all aspects of the field—from performance management to adult learning to corporate culture. Integrating cutting-edge research and innovative management practice, this library of titles will serve as an essential resource for human resource professionals, educators, students, and managers in all types of organizations.

The series editorial board includes leading academics and practitioners whose insights are shaping the theory and application of human resource development and organizational design.

Contents

List of Figures

List of Tables

Acknowledgments

The process of creating a book touches many lives, and many lives touch our own as well; it takes almost a community of diverse input and work. We would like to express our thanks to Perseus Publishing, especially Nick Philipson and Arlinda Shtuni. We are grateful to Hallie Preskill and Jerry Gilley for their interest and behind-the-scenes work. This book would never have happened without all of the individuals who participated in our research, and we especially want to thank Steve Preskill, Paul Shirley, and Robert Boverie. Several of our students were instrumental to this book and deserve special mention and thanks. First, Eileen Allison, for her painstaking proofreading and detective work. Rhonda Neel and Wendy Darnell spent hours working with the data and helped us make sense of it. Julia Mummert was always happy to track down another case study, write thank-you notes, or go to the library for us, and Sheryl Evans provided the artistic flair we needed.

Patricia's Acknowledgments

I want to thank my students who helped with this research and had to listen to me talk endlessly about passionate work.

I would like to thank all the members of my family. I am grateful to my husband, Blaine Henderson, for his love and support. He has always been there for me and I stand on his shoulders. My appreciation goes out to my son, Brian Saab, for providing me with laughter and love, and to my daughters, Elizabeth and Marie Henderson, for loving me through thick and thin and for all their patience. I am so passionate about my children and they continually transform and amaze me. Also my brothers and sisters, especially Sharon Valdes, who takes such good care of Mom and has been understanding about the time I have spent on this research and book. And to Betsy Boverie, for the many real and phone hugs that she has provided when they were most needed. I owe so much to my late father, Robert "Pete" Boverie, who instilled me with passion through his example and guidance. I especially want to thank my mother, Mary Eileen Boverie, for handing down so many of her wonderful gifts—gifts such as laughter, joy, wisdom, and her Irish passion. I also thank my "adopted family," the Kroths—Lana, Shane, and Piper—for lending me Michael this past year.

Last, I want to thank Michael. The enthusiasm and encouragement he gave me to follow my dream and his diligence in keeping me together has brought us here. He is a rare person, full of passion and love. He has taught me so much in this process and I am a different and better person as a result of working with him.

Michael's Acknowledgments

I want to thank my students as well. I've learned so much about passion from their stories. I also wish to thank my friends and colleagues at Public Service Company of New Mexico who have always been supportive, even when my top priority became this book.

My friend Stanley Weinstein has been a constant source of insight, not only about passionate work but also about life itself. He has been a true friend, giving support, encouragement, and thoughtful advice.

I want to thank Blaine, Elizabeth, and Marie Henderson for making me feel welcome and at home each time I came over to work on this book. I have enjoyed many meals and spent dozens of evenings, Saturdays, and Sundays at their house over the last couple of years. I appreciate their friendly acceptance of my presence in their lives.

My family has remained my constant supporters even when lawns didn't get mowed, when weekends were focused on writing rather than on family time, and when they had to do more because I had to do less. My son Shane has helped me in more ways than he knows. My daughter Piper has been a constant source of happiness for me. My wife Lana lives a life of passion, and inspires me every day.

My mother, Jane Kroth, has been a shoulder to cry on when times were truly difficult. She is always there when I need her, as are my brother and sisters, and the rest of my family. My dad, Roger Kroth, well, I'm dedicating this book to him. He exemplifies the true meaning of passionate work.

I have been privileged to work with a truly remarkable person on this book. Patricia started as my teacher nearly a decade ago, became a colleague after graduation, and over the course of writing this book has become a confidante, a close friend, and now we have a business together. She has become a true partner over the course of our relationship. She is someone I watch with admiration. She lives her life with true passion and there is no one I would rather travel down this 'passionate work' path with than her.

Prologue

We first began working together in the University of New Mexico's Training and Learning Technologies program in 1992. Patricia became Michael's academic adviser and subsequently his dissertation chairperson. In 1997, Michael graduated with a Ph.D. in what is now called UNM's Organizational Learning and Technologies program in the College of Education. During that time we discovered that we were both interested in doing further research related to organizational and individual transformation.

Patricia's areas of expertise are in the fields of individual, team, and organizational learning and she has consulted with numerous organizations over the years. She has done considerable research in the area of risk-taking, self-efficacy, and adult learning processes. Both of us had worked in large organizations and knew the opportunities and the problems that are involved. Consequently, we were interested in emancipatory, transformational learning for employees in organizations.

One day in 1999, we were talking about research and Patricia said that she had always been interested in the topic of passion, that she had always been a passionate person, and had wondered what caused people to become, to lose, and to regain their passion for work. Michael immediately saw how research in passionate work related to his interest in life mission and helping workers develop personal power to take control of their own futures. We saw the potential of this research; our imaginations were fired. Our decision to study passion and work was born that day. All the forces seemed to come together for us in a powerful way to lead us to our study of passionate work. Our research began immediately.

This research has been rewarding to us, yet time consuming. During the last couple of years we have conducted numerous presentations on passionate work, consulted with organizations, and been involved in other passionate work–related research. We could have stopped there but we seemed driven to share our message with a larger audience, thus the decision to write this book.

Our families, although supportive, have had to spend many nights and weekends by themselves while we type away, revising again and again. Why didn't we quit? The answer is simple—we believe in passionate work. We believe in living passionate lives. This work is deeply meaningful to us. We come from different backgrounds that prepared us for this work, but our diverse experiences led us to the same conviction. We are convinced that individuals can make quantum improvements to the quality of their lives and the productivity of their organizations if they will seek the means for living and working passionately. Likewise, organizations can increase productivity if they support a passionate workplace.

Why did we write this book? That's a worthy question to ask anyone writing about something intended to affect other people's lives. Between us, we have over forty years of experience in organizational development, consulting, training, teaching, communication, and human resources. As professors, we have seen hundreds of people return to school in midcareer. Many times these adults are looking for something meaningful to do with their lives. As organizational consultants, we have observed too many of the living dead—people who come to work as human beings on Monday morning and who then merely exist until being reborn Friday at 5:00. We've seen organizations that create conditions for exciting, interesting work, and we've seen too much of the opposite, organizations that drag down employees and make them feel and behave in less than human ways.

We started researching this issue of passionate work because we've both experienced it, arriving at passionate work from different paths, and we wanted to find out how others have created it for themselves. Intuitively, and from our own experience, we knew it was possible to develop passion, but we wanted to find out how anyone could make his or her life exciting, meaningful, and important. We wanted to share what we've learned with others by writing this book.

To understand the lens through which we see this material, it is helpful to know something about us.

Patricia's Story

I have always been a passionate person. I can trace it at least as far back to when I was five years old. Passion has been a mainstay—whether it got me in trouble, interfered with my life in disastrous ways, or led me to my life's work. Passion, by itself, can be detrimental, and it took me a long time to learn to temper it with thought, reflection, and reason.

As an adult I found myself a single parent, working in a male-dominated traditional banking environment. I was the director for Human Resource Development and an officer of a large bank. At first I was interested and motivated, but soon found the work unsatisfying for a number of reasons. First I was appalled at how women were perceived and treated in this corporate environment. Also, the strict cultural demands of the Texas "Good Ole Boy" system began to wear on my motivation. It wasn't too long before my more passionate, creative, and free-spirited nature rebelled and I found myself looking for more out of life. But at this point I couldn't just jump into the next fun thing. I was thirty-one years old and needed to do some real soul searching to discover what I wanted to do. If I were going to change jobs and potentially disrupt my six-year-old son's life, I wanted to be sure about what I did next.

Up to this time I had worked at a variety of jobs: car driver for a dealership, legal secretary, bookkeeper, leadership coordinator, trainer, human resources director, film and video producer, waitress, restaurant owner, salesperson, and the list goes on. I had taken jobs because I was bored, needed more money, or was offered opportunities I couldn't resist. I had two degrees, a bachelor's in business administration and a master's in clinical psychology. I had worked part-time and full-time while I was in school, usually two to three jobs at a time. In these various workplaces I had witnessed many people who hated their work, who felt trapped in unfulfilling jobs, and saw the almost total disregard of some organizations to the plight of their employees. I was especially distressed by how women and minorities were treated and wanted to work to change the system in some way. But I hadn't really considered what my life mission was—what I was destined to do.

I began deep self-reflection, examining where I had been, what I liked doing, and what my "gifts" were. I realized that I was most at home in an academic environment—in the world of ideas. I loved teaching and helping adults grow, develop, and transform. It became clear that I should apply for doctoral programs.

My first choice was the University of Texas at Austin and when I received my acceptance letter, all the tasks that I had envisioned as major barriers melted away. Up until then I had imagined moving my son, pets, and household to another city as too major a change. Suddenly, I couldn't wait to get started on the move. I had to quit my respectable, stable position, and start packing. I had no place to live, no money in the bank, no job waiting for me, and family, friends, and an ex-husband who wanted me to stay put. But I was finally going to be on course—to fulfill my life mission, to follow my passion, and nothing could hold me back.

That was fourteen years ago and I haven't regretted those decisions once in all that time. I wake up each day looking forward to going to work, I come alive when I get to teach, and I spend most of my free time working. I am truly passionate about being a college professor—it is what I was destined to do.

Now I want to help others find their passion, their mission, and their destiny. I want to make going to work each day life-generating and satisfying for others. We all have gifts that make us special and unique. I want to help others find their gifts and help organizations learn to honor those talents and strengths and use them to become passionate workplaces.

Michael's Story

I have worked for one company almost my entire career. I got a position with the electric company because I needed a job to support my family. I had graduated from college a year and a half earlier with a degree in theater arts. With a wife and a child I needed work and I sure wasn't getting offers from Broadway or Hollywood, so I took a secure job in our state's largest electric utility. The job was in personnel, in which I had no background or particular interest.

Over twenty-two years later, I was still employed by the same company. Nearly every day I drove the same route to work, parked in one of the same parking lots, and then walked down the same alley to enter our building. Five days a week times fifty weeks a year for twenty-two and a half years comes to over 5,600 times. And that's just going one way.

During the first decade I made rapid progress through the company. I became involved in work I really enjoyed. I was doing primarily public and community relations work. Executives took me under their wings and encouraged me. The work was exciting. The times were heady. The future was bright.

The next five years were just the opposite. I went from a young up-and-comer working in the executive offices to a person who—in my view at the time—the corporation didn't really want. The company went through a major downsizing. The leaders I had followed and cared the most about were leaving or would be leaving soon. Executives who remained couldn't promise me anything, certainly nothing important, and in my mind, perceived me as part of the departing regime. I turned cynical about the company. I changed from a guy who made things happen to a survivor.

For years I survived. Survived layoffs and survived reorganizations. Then came the ultimate slap in the face—I was impacted (our term for being laid off). I even survived that by being hired into another department.

During that period of time I did some real soul searching about myself. I looked excruciatingly inside . . . and found myself wanting. I dug deep to ask myself what I wanted to do with my life and what would make it meaningful.

I resolved to dedicate my life to helping people take responsibility for their lives and not depend on an organization for their success. After all, I had abdicated responsibility for myself to others for many years, to my regret.

I wrote a mission statement in my journal on January 1, 1994: "My mission is to help individuals and groups fulfill their full potential. . . . I am particularly interested in helping people develop a purpose in their lives and a life of meaningfulness; to help the 'living dead' awake and walk." That essentially remains my main purpose today—to help individuals develop personal power in their lives. I've since learned a lot about not taking life so seriously and the wonderfulness of living with both joy and meaningfulness, and so my mission has evolved into helping individuals attain their own passion for living. I've been to hell myself and it's not a pretty place.

The few years have been increasingly exciting and meaningful. I have been doing work I enjoy with people I like and admire. Over the last twenty-two and a half years I have been atop the peaks and deep into the valleys. My love for work has truly waxed and waned. I'm at a peak right now. I thought and thought about the future and came to the conclusion that, even though my job gave me great satisfaction, I would never realize my full potential by staying where I was at and doing what I was doing. So . . . April 30, 2001, was my last day to work for the company where I had been for twenty-two years.

On May 1, 2001, I started my new career at Boverie, Kroth, & Associates, dedicated to individual and organizational transformation and to passionate work. I am scared and excited at the same time. I am thrilled about the prospects of continuing our research and of working with people and organizations so that I can understand passionate work more deeply and more usefully. I want to help people to develop passion in their own lives. I want to support organizations that are willing to create environments where people love to come to work. As I write this the future lies before me. One thing I know for sure—today I am truly alive.

The Voices in Our Book

As we worked together to create this book perhaps our most difficult task was to create a voice for the book. We began with quite different perspectives and writing styles. We haggled over whether the text should be in the first person or third person, whether it should be written more "academically" or more "popularly," and whether the target audience was individuals or organizations. We thought that we had an important message for both employees and their employers. As the work evolved, however, the need to make those decisions seemed to evaporate. The work began to take on a life of its own. The voice that has emerged is no longer Patricia and no longer Michael. It is Patricia and Michael together. We decided to write this manuscript with an equal emphasis on what individuals could do and what organizations could do because in many ways they became inseparable to us. We both believe that some organizations maintain onerous, oppressive working conditions, and we believe also in their power to provide uplifting, inspiring conditions. We both believe in the primacy of the person, and of the moral, ethical, and spiritual imperative to honor the humanness in every worker. We oppose anything—societal, organizational, interpersonal, or cultural—that degrades the human spirit or promotes dependency, misery, or hopelessness. We deeply believe that organizations will be successful, in the long run, to the extent that they support, develop, and respect their employees. The voice of this book speaks from this worldview.

The voices of this book go well beyond Patricia and Michael, however. We have had the marvelous opportunity to learn about passion from coworkers, students, leaders, and employees. Some people who allowed us to use their names we have identified for you. We didn't ask for the names of others you will read about. Some wanted to share their stories, but not their names. We learned from each person and we pay tribute to their lives. Sometimes their honesty was agonizingly painful to hear, and sometimes their lives made our own seem tepid in comparison. They are the true voice of this book.

The Fire Transforms

The fire of our lives burns brightly. The process of working together has taught us much about life, about learning, and about collaboration. Together we have created something that we realize neither of us could have imagined or developed individually. We have been transformed individually and as a team through this research-and-writing process. We feel so strongly about this lifework that we will continue researching passionate work and sharing what we learn with individuals and organizations through the company we've created, Boverie, Kroth, & Associates. We have developed a sense of mission regarding passionate work that seems to have a life of its own.

How You Can Help

As we continue to study passionate work we want to hear about passionate work. If you know of an organization that has created a passionate work environment, a leader who is passionate about her or his work, or an employee who exemplifies passion at work, please let us know. Send your stories to us at pboverie@spinn.net or michaelkroth@msn.com.

Introduction to Passion and Work

We may affirm absolutely that nothing great in the world
has been accomplished without passion.

—HEGEL, Philosophy of History, 1832

The Time Is Now

Individuals today have an unprecedented opportunity to create careers
that will provide continual learning, challenge, and reward. For centuries, the balance of power has been in the hands of the organization. If
one worker didn't fit in, the next one would do, or the next one, or the
next one. The scarcity of labor is shifting the balance of power to those
who are selling talent and skills. The time is ripe for people who have the
will and the courage to fashion passionate career paths for themselves.

Organizations today are at risk because of the escalating demand for
talent and the prospect of a reduced supply of labor. There has never
been a more important time for leaders to develop working environments that are humane, challenging, and rewarding. There has never
been a more important time for leaders to create places where individuals come to work each day charged up and excited about the work they
are asked to do—places where people are passionate about their work.

Business and organizational leaders may find it peculiar to read a
book about passion. Historically, emotions at work have been discouraged, been made fun of, or trivialized. The vanilla, stoic, organizational

man of decades past did not tolerate the diversity or the display of emotions. Showing fear, joy, anguish, or love was a sign of weakness, even though emotions are part of the natural human condition. And yet passion is the fire, the drive, and the energy that motivates humankind.

Passion is loaded with emotion, with desire, with action, and with thought. Passion is at the root of creative genius, personal transformation, and notable events. Passion is emotional energy; it stimulates life and energizes individuals to work toward goals. It propels willpower, gives one boldness, and is an outlet for emotional, physical, and creative release. New products, new ideas, creative ways to deliver services, inventions, and scientific discoveries are produced because someone or some organization is passionate.

Yet over time we have tried to make the workplace an arena without emotion. We want the outcome of passionate work, but we don't want employees to have emotions at work. Taking passion out of the workplace creates halls of despair, corridors of the living dead.

We need a new conception of the workplace. Instead of squashing emotions, we need to channel them. Instead of chastising the passion in employees, we need to help people to understand what they love to do. We need to have a workplace where employees are not confused because we say we want them to be loyal and hardworking and yet ask them to check their desire, their humanity, at the door.

The Purpose of the Book

Although many writers have written about passion for work, no one that we know of has drawn upon the concepts of interpersonal passion—love, desire, intimacy, and romance—and applied them to work. This book describes our research and the linkages that we have found between motivation, work, and learning. Learning, our research revealed, is embedded throughout everything related to passion for work. The concepts in this book are anchored in our research with real people, related research and literature, and relationships we have found with relevant existing theory.

The purpose of this book is to give individuals and organizations the tools to create passionate work environments for themselves. This book is intended to improve people's lives. Its first purpose is to give individuals specific processes that can be used to find, develop, and maintain work they can be passionate about. Its second purpose is to give organizations specific processes that can be used to develop and maintain passionate work environments.

This book is written for several key audiences. It has direct application for the average worker—any person who feels stuck in her or his job, who is interested in looking for something more interesting or worthwhile, or who loves their job and wants that love to continue. Employees looking for new vocational venues will find the material interesting, informative, and useful. It will be a valuable tool for executives and other organizational leaders attempting to create highly motivating work environments. HRD professionals will be able to draw upon these ideas to help their organizations and clients develop passionate work. Even employees close to retirement will find the book useful because it will give them a framework for thinking about their future.

This is a book that presents a philosophy of life and a philosophy of work that will increase the enjoyment and the meaning of both life and work. It is a book about the indispensable necessity of passion for personal and organizational success.

Individuals

Philosophers, theologians, career consultants, organizational gurus, psychologists, and just about anyone looking into the relationship of work to individual satisfaction have made the point that finding work that is meaningful and enjoyable leads to mental, physical, spiritual, and emotional health.

In many ways, work dominates your life. Just consider the actual time that work consumes for the average person. If you add actual work time, travel time, and preparation time, your job takes more of your time than anything else. That doesn't count the time spent thinking about work or being distracted about work when at home or being involved in other activities. Managing work time to its fullest is essential for a fully balanced life.

The responsibility for creating passionate work cannot be entrusted to another person. It resides within the individual. Yet it is often handed over to fate or to other people. Ask almost any group of Baby Boomers how their careers developed and part of that group will say that they stumbled into their first job out of school. They just happened into their first job and, moreover, they are still in the same line of work, and even at the same company, twenty-five years later. "A survey reported in a US popular psychology magazine revealed that up to 40 percent of the population had 'drifted' into a career and less than a quarter had personally chosen their line of work" (Simpson 1999: 31). Many people do not intentionally choose their careers. Consequently, they are at the mercy of their employers. It has been said that a person without a goal is used by someone who has one. This takes on added significance when an individual's livelihood is at stake.

This book will put the reins of personal agency more firmly in the hands of the individual women and men who want to carve out a meaningful career path. It will give insight to those who have more limited options and help them to explore useful alternatives.

Organizations

Now is the time for organizations to find ways to tap into human potential. Capturing the hearts and minds of Generation X is one driver. The global marketplace is another. The risk of ignoring the importance of attracting and retaining key talent is huge. McKinsey and Company conducted a year-long study involving seventy-seven companies and nearly 6,000 business executives, and came to the conclusion that talent will be the most important—and rare—corporate resource in the next twenty years. Their report "The War for Talent" (Chambers et al. 1998) is a wake-up call for leaders thinking strategically about their future. With a drought of labor forecasted, what organizations consider "strategic" talent will expand. It will include much more than highly visible executives. Labor of all kinds will be at a premium. Professions and crafts that experienced a glut of labor just a few years ago are already experiencing shortages, and organizations are beginning to beg employees to stay.

Successful organizations will attract, develop, and retain talent in every part of the company. One element of the employee value proposition is how meaningful and fun the work is in a particular company. Companies wishing to compete will pay close attention to what motivates their employees. Often given lip service in the past, keeping employees charged up about their work will become a strategic objective. Companies that do it well over time will find it a source of sustainable competitive advantage.

Passion isn't just critical in the world of corporate competition. It is just as important in public sector organizations. HRD professionals and leaders in any organization must be attentive to what fuels an employee's passion. Fried (1995), in his book *The Passionate Teacher,* relates the importance of passion to teaching.

> Yet as I look into hundreds of classrooms, watch teachers working with all kinds of students, when I ask myself what makes the greatest difference in the quality of student learning—it is a teacher's passion that leaps out. More than knowledge of subject matter. More than variety of teaching techniques. More than being well-organized, or friendly, or funny, or fair. (16)

Embedding programs and processes inside the organization that energize employees will be the sine qua non for future success.

What Is Passion?

We all experience passion by virtue of being human. Passion evokes images of deep commitment to another person, to an idea, or to a cause. Every person has the capacity for passion and yet many do not lead passionate lives. The passion has been beaten out of them by society, or their work, or by significant people in their lives.

Passion. The word itself conjures up images of steamy romance between two lovers, of fighting for one's country or for a worthy cause, of an inventor working day and night to discover something new, of starting a new business and seeing one's dream come true, or of raising wonderful children. The word passion evokes images of adventure, excitement, love, inspiration, and challenge. We long for ecstasy, intensity, and thrills. Passion is part of the human condition, and so can be a part of anyone's life.

People want passion in their lives. Popular magazines, soap operas, movies, romantic novels, sports events, plays, and music all play upon this desire that resides deep within every person. Some people create artificial, dangerous highs in their lives to meet this need. Some people lust after the lifestyles of people who had the courage to follow their dreams. Hopeless people anesthetize themselves to the pain of dreary lives by participating in disparaging coffee break gossip about other vital, enthusiastic coworkers. Passion is coveted by those who observe it and cherished by those who live it.

We are rapt watching an Olympic champion achieve her dream, and wonder why we gave up our own. Where did we lose our dreams? We couldn't wait to start the new job after school, and here we sit so many years later, just putting in time until the company will allow us to retire. The opposite of love is not hate—it is apathy. Apathy dulls our senses, breaks our spirits, and makes us forget our dreams. Passion does not include apathy but very often it includes pain.

Passion has several definitions, including: "intense, driving, or overmastering feeling," "ardent affection: love," "a strong liking for or devotion to some activity, object, or concept" (Webster 1979: 831) and words with similar meaning include fervor, ardor, enthusiasm, or zeal. Passion experienced this way feels like the mountains singing, the oceans erupting, or the skies laughing—it is the ultimate high. But passion isn't so simple. The origin of the word passion comes from *passio,* or suffering (Webster 1979). Suffering, or pain, is a very real part of passion and one of the reasons many people are not willing to expose themselves to it. Perhaps the easiest way to observe both the high and low of passion is in sports. It's the championship game and two teams have extended themselves beyond anything they've ever done before. The final buzzer goes off. One team celebrates, with tears in their eyes. The other team does not, also with tears in their eyes. Or worse, one player goes to the absolute limit and fails, letting his or her team (and perhaps even country) down. You can almost feel their pain yourself.

The duel pain and joy of passion extends to every part of the human condition. Imagine a play opening on Broadway. Every person involved—from producer and director to actors, crew, stage manager, and scene designer—throughout the entire company, is committed to its success. The play is panned the first night out and closes soon after. Each person is devastated. You can conjure up countless situations where passion produces both joy and pain. People are often unwilling to be vulnerable either as employees or in other parts of their lives. The pursuit of passion requires taking risks that could result in pain. So instead of feeling pain—these people feel nothing.

Passion is observable. In an individual it can be seen in a twinkle in the eye, a lilt to the step, an enthusiastic conversation about a project or a person, or an unwavering commitment to a goal. It can manifest itself in loud, voluble, emotional enthusiasm. Or it might be much more subtle and quieter, but no less focused or intense because it is less extravagant. "People who love their work exhibit enormous energy, a positive state of mind, and a sense of vision and purpose. They realize that what they are doing fits into a larger picture and can see how what they do makes a difference in the world as a whole" (Jaffe and Scott 1988: 69).

Passion may be experienced in differing ways but, if it is there, it is palpable. One person we talked to, Kitty Leslie, said "I define true passion as having such a strong and consistent presence in your life that all those close to you suspect it, even if you've never voiced it in great detail." Southwest Airlines is a good example of a passionate organization. The people in this company seem to be so passionate that they have been described as "nuts."

> Are these people nuts? Well, if being nuts means they are crazy about the company they work for, the answer is a resounding yes! If being nuts means they are extremely enthusiastic about what they do, the answer is again yes! If being nuts means being intensely involved, even obsessed, these people are definitely nuts about providing legendary customer service. If a nut is someone who is fanatically committed to a cause, these people clearly fit the description. The people of Southwest Airlines are radicals and revolutionaries—committed to the cause of keeping fares low to make air travel affordable for everyone. (Freiberg and Freiberg 1996: 3)

For individuals, passion resides internally and may be expressed to others. For organizations, passion is the cumulative, emotional effect of every employee interacting with his or her work and with each other.

Passion may be great joy or great pain. Perhaps the best way of understanding passion is to use a powerful metaphor—fire—to describe it.

Fire Metaphor

> *Your reason and your passion are the rudder and the sails*
> *of your seafaring soul.*
> *If either your sails or your rudder be broken you can but*
> *toss and drift, or else be held at a standstill in mid-seas.*
> *For reason, ruling alone, is a force confining; and passion,*
> *unattended, is a flame that burns to its own destruction.*
> *Therefore let your soul exalt your reason to the height of*
> *passion, that it may sing;*
> *And let it direct your passion with reason, that your*
> *passion may live through its own daily resurrection, and*
> *like the phoenix rise above its own ashes.*
> —KAHLIL GIBRAN, *The Prophet* (1995, pp. 50–51)

Fire is one of the most descriptive metaphors for passion. Many of the words used to characterize passion also define fire. Whyte (1994: 77) has said that "At work or at home we are *fired* by enthusiasm, *branded* with cowardice, and *inflamed* with sexual desire. We find ourselves in the *heat* of the moment, or *burned* by circumstances. We look for the creative *spark,* long for human *warmth,* and in times of need, call on the *fire* in our bellies. And bereft of these, we are left with only *ashes.*"

Fire transforms, destroys, creates, and forges bonds of infinite strength. Fire can burn out of control, can delicately melt something ugly to create something beautiful, and can be snuffed out. Without fire we are primitive, we are cold, and we are inert.

In its purest form, passion creates the heat that transforms lives. When someone is passionate enough about his work, he becomes his work, in the best sense. The following story illustrates the depth to which passion can burn inside a person.

There is an ancient Chinese story of an old master potter who attempted to develop a new glaze for his porcelain vases. It became the central focus of his life. Every day he tended the flames of his kilns to a white heat, controlling the temperature to an exact degree. Every day he experimented with the chemistry of the glazes he applied, but still he could not achieve the beauty he desired and imagined was possible in the glaze. Finally, having tried everything, he decided his meaningful life was over and walked into the molten heat of a fully fired kiln. When his assistants opened up the kiln and took out the vases, they found the glaze on the vases the most exquisite they had ever encountered. The master himself had disappeared into his creations. (Whyte 1994: 114)

People who are passionate about their work either seem to be on fire, blazing out of control, or to have the intentional, quiet, white-hot intensity of a beautiful glassmaker. Passionate teachers sometimes burn with such intensity, and sometimes "[passion] bellows forth with thunder and eloquence" (Fried 1995: 17). Even when the intensity makes people uneasy, it is what separates them from others. Again, David Whyte in *The Heart Aroused* (1994), says "Work is the very fire where we are baked to perfection" (115).

Passion can, like an uncontained forest fire, burn out of control, leaving organizational and individual devastation behind. However, organizations and people, like the mythical phoenix, can rise from the ashes as if new. As fire destroys, it may also transform. Tempering passion with reason produces creativity, energy, excitement, and results.

People who are passionate about their work can also burn out if the organization does not feed their flame with recognition, rewards, new learning, and support for risk-taking and challenge. Without this organizational support the fire inside a person may smolder out, or the individual may move on to places where her fire can be fed. How many people burned brightly for a while, only to see "organizational firefighters" douse the flame? Reigniting that flame is more difficult for some than for others, but the source of fire always resides in each of us, ready for the match to strike.

Organizational passion can also supplant individual passion. An organization may consume the person who has little heat. If one's internal, individual fire does not burn strongly enough, personal dreams may turn into ashes. "If we do give up our personal desires and passions hoping to get above it all, we almost always find ourselves substituting the passions and desires of someone more charismatic for our own, and wake up later to find ourselves in their thrall" (Whyte 1994: 77). It is two flames—organizational and individual—burning together, blending into one, that create the blazing power of fusion.

The fire of passion consists of two important elements—the pure joy of working and the meaningfulness of that work. The next section will describe these two aspects of passion.

What Are the Qualities of Passion?

> Your vocation is "the place where your great joy, and society's great needs, meet."
> —FREDERICK BUECHNER (1993: 119)

People we have interviewed described the feeling of passion as:

A feeling of loving what I do.
Consumed, longing, placing a high value on something.
Being positive and excited. Looking forward to each day.
Excited about being with that individual or performing that job's tasks.
Feeling fired up about something or someone and wanting to share that feeling with others.
A feeling of elation and satisfaction leading to a desire to keep going even when I may begin to feel tired.
Feeling good about what you are doing and who you are with.
Excitement, a sense of mission, purpose, and single-mindedness that lasts for the duration of a project or endeavor (not "short-term").
Exciting, exhilarating, caring, loving, giving, refreshing.
Something that just takes over and gives me a great deal of pleasure.

Passion contains two interrelated qualities: (1) the pure joy and excitement of doing something that is enjoyable to do, and (2) meaningfulness, or caring deeply about something. Passion can be found in either, but to be fully engaged requires both. For example, a person might find the actual act of cleaning bedpans to be distasteful, but be passionate about doing it because he cares for patients and their health. Conversely, a person who enjoys being a ski bum may tire of it after a short while.

Passion is usually short-lived if enjoyment is not accompanied by meaning, and meaning without joy is often dreary duty or responsibility.

Fun, Enthusiasm, and Joy. A person who is passionate about another person loves to be with him or her. Each meeting is exciting, and even anticipating the meeting itself causes the heart to beat a bit faster. The couple finds each moment together rich, sensory, full of laughter, and fresh. New relationships are particularly full of excitement, because everything involves mutual discovery. Couples in long-term relationships who maintain their passion find enjoyment in spending time together, have mutual activities that they have fun doing, and are enthusiastic about their lives together.

For work to be passionate it must also be fun, exciting, and enjoyable. Many people have lost this, and with it their capacity for passionate work. Understanding what it is we love to do and then finding ways to pursue that work is an important part of living passionately. After a seminar one person said, "Thank you for the information. I wish I'd known this before, because I've worked in this job for thirty years, and for thirty years I've hated it." Hated it! What a sad, sad commentary on a person's life. Over the years, fun and work have been considered mutually exclusive terms. Various religious denominations focused entirely on duty and responsibility—work wasn't supposed to be fun. In corporate cubicles today one can hear the teasing phrase, "Oh, you're just having too much fun!" as if having fun were exceptional and not quite acceptable. That has been changing.

Savvy, successful organizations have recognized the importance of fun and excitement at work. Peters and Waterman's study found that America's best-run companies create enthusiasm. "A final correlation among the excellent companies is the extent to which their leaders unleash excitement" (1982: 291). "The theme of fun in business runs through a great deal of the excellent companies research," they say. "Leaders and managers like what they do and they get enthusiastic about it" (247).

Having fun can, but doesn't necessarily have to be, crazy, outlandish, or rife with practical jokes. It can take the form of more smiles, mutual support, making work a game or a challenge, or finding creative ways to provide recognition.

Joy is a critical component of passion. Laurence Boldt, in his book *How to Find the Work You Love* (1996), says that "As much as integrity to conscience and service to others, joy is an absolute requirement of a life's work. Man was not made for drudgery or tedium. Life is a thing to be tasted, celebrated, and enjoyed. The great joy in work is in self-expression, following the way of your natural talents" (96). We weren't meant for monotony. We were designed for variety and challenge. One of the most quoted writers on this topic is Joseph Campbell, who talks about finding the life work that gives "bliss." "If you follow your bliss, you put yourself on a kind of track that has been there all the while, waiting for you, and the life that you ought to be living is the one you are living. Wherever you are—if you are following your bliss, you are enjoying that refreshment, that life within you, all the time" (Campbell 1988: 113).

What makes you happy? His Holiness the Dalai Lama says, "I believe that the very purpose of our life is to seek happiness" (1998: 13). On the whole, unhappy people are less productive, less sociable, and less helpful. Happy people are generally more productive, enjoy life more, and are more creative and more loving. Making the commitment to be happy is a decision we make. The steps to achieve happiness entail learning about what makes us happy and then building a life around that self-awareness.

Shawn Shepherd, a development officer and part-time play director talked to us about her work with plays. "Engaged as I was in the work necessary to craft a professional theater production—eighteen-hour days for the three-week period that Equity provides for to mount a play—I never felt the exhaustion that normally accompanies this demanding schedule. Instead, each day became more of a joy, with increasing energy through opening night and the full run of the show." When we feel happy we are fully in the moment, content, care about the result, and enjoy what we are doing. Willa Cather expressed it well in *My Ántonia*. "That is happiness; to be dissolved into something complete and great. When it comes to one, it comes as naturally as sleep" (1954: 14).

Meaningfulness.   Think, for a moment, about how it feels to do meaningless work. Sisyphus, in ancient mythology, was the wisest of the mortals. After angering the gods he was assigned the eternal task of rolling a rock up a hill. As he approached the summit, each time the rock rolled back to its original position before it reached the top. Can you imagine the toil of pushing that rock up time after time, straining and stressing, only to see all of your work go for naught? Can you imagine Sisyphus's thoughts as he walked down that hill in preparation for the next attempt? Can you sense the torment he felt? Do you feel like Sisyphus as you drive to work each morning?

What would it be like to produce a wonderful product, only to see your supervisor toss it in the trash? Even if you enjoyed the process of creating this product, how passionate would you be about your work if this happened every day? How would you feel?

Knowing that we do something of importance is an essential part of love. "When we love something it is of value to us, and when something is of value to us we spend time with it, time enjoying it and time taking care of it" (Peck 1978: 22). Loved work must be valuable and meaningful, or it will ultimately be perceived as superficial and transitory, as fool's gold rather than the genuine article. Researcher Daniel Yankelovich found that employees are seeking "meaning, growth, personal challenge, and intimate relationships in work and personal experiments" (Jaffe and Scott 1988: 14). People seek fulfillment by doing work they view as important.

We want work to make a difference. We feel strongly about the things we do that will change people's lives, improve the world, and leave a legacy for others. Our research confirms that it is not merely the enjoyment of work, but also the meaningfulness of work that produces passion. One woman told us she experiences passion for her work "by feeling needed and that I am contributing to something I think is important." Justin Trager, a former political campaign worker, told us, "I believed so strongly in the value and importance of my work, that I sacrificed almost every other component of my life. . . . Even the little interaction I had with family and friends reinforced my experiences because they were being supportive of my developing career."

Studs Terkel, in the introduction to his book *Working* (1972) said that work is:

> about a search, too, for daily meaning as well as daily bread, for recognition as well as cash, for astonishment rather than torpor; in short, for a sort of life rather than a Monday through Friday sort of dying. Perhaps

immortality, too, is part of the quest. To be remembered was the wish, spoken and unspoken, of the heroes and heroines of this book. (xi)

For many, spirituality is a necessary component of meaningfulness.
Spiritual leaders from earliest times have taught that work is a manifes-
tation of our inner or spiritual selves. In his book *The Reinvention of
Work*, Matthew Fox says that "Work comes from inside out; work is the
expression of our soul, our inner being . . . it is the expression of the
Spirit at work in the world through us" (1994: 5). Today, many people
are engaged not just in finding the meaning of work, but in finding the
meaning of life itself.

In *Work and the Human Spirit*, John Scherer describes work as a critical element of future success.

> The huge challenges facing the workplace today are not going to be over-
> come with new management theories or motivational tips and techniques.
> Even such radical organizational surgery as re-engineering by itself will
> not be enough. I happen to believe that we are in a crisis which must be
> approached as something so profound, so fundamental, so universal, that
> it can only be resolved at the level of the human spirit. (1993: 7)

Scherer says:

> What it takes for *companies* to survive is also what it takes for *individuals*
> who make them up to survive. The highest goals of any business can best
> be realized by awakening and nurturing the human spirit of the people
> who comprise it—its leaders, its employees, and even its customers. (5–6)

Yet organizations either overlook or trivialize this inner need. In *Leading
with Soul* Bolman and Deal say that "Most management and leadership
programs ignore or demean spirit. They desperately need an infusion of
poetry, literature, music, art, theater, history, philosophy, dance and
other forms that are full of spirit" (1995: 167–168). Leaders who recognize this human need tap into core human qualities that revitalize lives
and organizations. "Leading with soul returns us to ancient spiritual ba-
sics—reclaiming the enduring human capacity that gives our lives pas-

sion and purpose" (6). "Perhaps we lost our way," Bolman and Deal remind us, "when we forgot that the heart of leadership lies in the hearts of leaders"(6).

Organizations that tap into their employees' deepest sense of personal purpose and values will harvest a wealth of passion focused on reaching mutual goals. Organizations that force employees to act in opposition to their beliefs will lobotomize their spirit and harvest withering hearts and chopped-up minds. Those organizations with a strong set of core beliefs and a true sense of mission and vision, have the discipline to align corporate incentives and programs around them, and then hire people who also share the same values, will be the ones that attract and retain the best and the brightest talent in the future.

Meaningfulness may be overlooked by organizations. They may assume that money is ample reward for individuals or think that having fun is sufficient. Yet according to Viktor Frankl, striving to find meaning in life is one's primary motivational force. "This meaning is unique and specific in that it must and can be fulfilled by him alone . . . " (1984: 105). Frankl, writing about the horrors of living in a concentration camp, talked about those whose suffering and death ". . . Bore witness to the fact that the last inner freedom cannot be lost. It can be said that they were worthy of their sufferings. . . . It is this spiritual freedom—which cannot be taken away—that makes life meaningful and purposeful" (75–76).

Passion involves meaningfulness and it involves enjoyment but does it make any difference? Why should employers care if people are passionate about their work? What importance does enjoyment have for employees? These issues are at the core of why passion is important.

Why Is Passion Important?

Passionate work, for individuals, is the difference between envisioning themselves as galley slaves, rowing and rowing and rowing in a physically, emotionally, spiritually, and mentally backbreaking environment; and envisioning themselves as fully human, creative, energetic, and enthusiastic individuals. Passionate work, for organizations, is the difference between lethargy, manipulation, management-employee separation, and "just tell me what to do" employees; and highly productive, problem-solving, tightly focused, idea generating employees. In either case, individual or organizational, which would you prefer?

It seems so simple. Go to work each day, make money, come home and enjoy it. Yet we cannot so neatly partition our lives. In *The Heart Aroused* David Whyte says ". . . while we think we are simply driving to work every morning to earn a living, the soul knows it is engaged in a life-or-death struggle for its existence" (1994: 80). Our work, in many ways, is the very essence of who we are. Tichy and Sherman, in describing how Jack Welch transformed General Electric, said:

> Work, inevitably, is an emotional experience: healthy people can't just drop their feelings off at home like a set of golf clubs. Yet management theory has long neglected this realm, and we are just beginning the search for ways to harness the vast power of workers' emotional energy. (1993: 64)

Although people have attempted to disassociate emotion from work, the reality is that one can no more do that than one can cut his heart out of his chest and still live. Numbing oneself to the emotion of work results in living death. According to Collins and Porras, visionary companies look to "keep alive that 'fire that burns from within' that impels people to keep pushing, to never be satisfied, and to always search for improvement" (1997: 187).

Organizations that view workers as things to be manipulated get only a small percentage of what a human being can contribute. People know when they are valued as human beings.

> For the many, there is a hardly concealed discontent. The blue-collar blues is no more bitterly sung than the white-collar moan. "I'm a machine," says the spot-welder. "I'm caged," says the bank teller, and echoes the hotel clerk. "I'm a mule," says the steelworker. "A monkey can do what I do," says the receptionist. "I'm less than a farm implement," says the migrant worker. "I'm an object," says the high-fashion model. Blue collar and white call upon the identical phrase: "I'm a robot." (Terkel 1972: xii)

In our research we have asked hundreds of people if there is a relationship between productivity and passion. The answer is always yes. Always. It isn't a one-to-one correlation. A person who doubles her passion for work may not achieve twice the productivity. There are too many intervening variables—supervisors who might get in the way, the lack of money, uncooperative coworkers, or obsolete equipment, as examples—to assure such a gain. All things being equal, however, increased passion results in increased productivity. Why? Because passionate people are more creative, exercise more discipline, exhibit more perseverance, work harder and longer, and inspire others to higher levels of performance.

If increasing passion is related to increasing productivity, is there an associated penalty for the lack of passion?

What Happens in the Absence of Passionate Environments?

Studs Terkel opens his book, *Working,* with these somber words.

> This book, being about work, is, by its very nature, about violence—to the spirit as well as to the body. It is about ulcers as well as accidents, about shouting matches as well as fistfights, about nervous breakdowns as well as kicking the dog around. It is, above all (or beneath all), about daily humiliations. To survive the day is triumph enough for the walking wounded among the great many of us. (Terkel 1972: xi)

Most people know, from personal experience or observation, the terrible toll that work can impose. In contrast to the uplifting, fulfilling, wondrous life work experienced by some, work for others sucks out the soul, destroys physically, creates psychological pain, or cracks the spirit. Work reduces these individuals to "human capital," or "assets," or "organizational slack," or "overhead," or "tools," or "resources" (as in how many resources can we throw at this problem?). Do you work "4–10s," or are on call perhaps "24-7"? Can we trust you to work from your home? Have you beat your head against organizational wall after wall after wall, only to find in the twilight of your career that the demographics are now allowing younger people to sprint by you, as your hands are tied to the shackles of a long-term benefit package?

For some, work isn't pain so much as the absence of pain, or any kind of feeling. Simpson, in *Working from the Heart,* says that "The tragedy is, many people's working lives become like their marriages where passion has been exchanged for comfort, security and predictability. Very safe, yes, very boring, certainly, and for many of us likely to precipitate a living death" (1999: 13).

The "living dead" is a term that seems to have become part of society's vocabulary. Naylor, Willimon, and Naylor, in their book *The Search for Meaning*, label their entire introduction "The Living Dead," and say, "Even though we live in a period of unprecedented prosperity, novelist Walker Percy warns that it is the Time of Thanatos—a time of the *living dead* in which 'people who seem to be living lives which are good by all sociological standards . . . somehow seem to be more dead than alive'" (12). "Many," they say, "who are physically alive appear to be spiritually, emotionally, and intellectually dead" (12).

Workers who have observed other coworkers being laid off can become mere survivors. Survivors exhibit little initiative. They just want to be told what to do and not to take any risks. Survivors don't test the waters and usually work only as hard as they have to work. Survivors play the organizational game to endure, not to thrive. Reflecting their perception that the organization doesn't care about its employees, they sometimes even sabotage the efforts of the organization and their coworkers. Survivors often have diminished self-esteem and resent organizations and their leaders.

Work without joy or meaning results in burnout, lifelessness, lack of creativity, and a dearth of initiative. From the individual's perspective, going to work each day in this mode is an attempt each day to survive. The goal is just to make it through eight hours until the clock says it's time to go. From the organization's perspective, huge amounts of productivity and unfulfilled results are left on the table, as worker ingenuity, drive, and collaborative spirit remain untapped.

Generation X and Passionate Work. One compelling reason for organizations to focus on creating passionate work environments is the emergence of Generation X as a dominant factor in the labor market. There are 44 million Generation Xers in the United States, compared with 77 million Baby Boomers many of whom are nearing the end of their careers. From a labor perspective it is becoming more and more of a seller's marketplace. In other words, the prospective seller—in this case a member of Generation X—will increasingly be able to set her or his own terms. Companies will be forced to create work environments where people actually want to work, to attract the talent they need to be successful. To look at it somewhat cynically, many organizations that have touted their desire to create humane work environments but haven't delivered the goods will be forced to do so for competitive reasons.

Consider the workers of the future to be "free agents." Organizations will be competing for talent much like professional sports teams bid for players and film producers vie for marquee stars. Increasingly portable benefits programs reinforce worker mobility. Although it is dangerous to make wholesale generalizations about any group of people, several attributes of Generation X employees seem to be common for many. They tend to be independent problem solvers, they look for immediate gratification, distrust institutions, recognize the need to continually learn and develop new skills, accept and even require change, and embrace diversity in all of its forms. They know that they are in demand (Bova and Kroth 1999).

What kind of workplaces will attract Generation X? None other than passionate environments. Places where it is exciting to work. Places where people support each other. Places where work makes a difference. Places where people are compensated based on their worth. Bova and Kroth found three themes related to hiring, nurturing, and mentoring Generation X employees over time:

Theme One: Work and the work environment must support continuing learning.
Theme Two: Mentors and organizational leaders must lead by example.
Theme Three: Generation X employees place major importance on having multidimensional lives. (1999: 12)

In another study, Bova and Kroth found that Generation X employees want an "atmosphere conducive to learning" and to "enjoy what I'm doing and also learn a lot of different things." Generation Xers want work to be constantly challenging. They want to be stretched. One GenX employee said she wanted the company to "move me around," and another said, "I have to be kept interested." Tasks should not be something "you've done a hundred million times." In terms of personal learning styles, Bova and Kroth found that action learning is most preferred by Generation X employees, followed by incidental learning, and then formal learning. Factors that facilitate the learning process are "the human touch, organizational scaffolding, high quality management, and special programs" (2001: 63) that promote learning. These programs might include job rotations, stretch assignments, task force leadership, mentoring, or new product development assignments. They conclude by saying that "Organizations wanting to capture the hearts of Generation X employees will make employee development a burning priority" (64).

The influence of Generation X goes far beyond its own members. The changing labor market will impact Baby Boomers. Because of the scarcity of talent, Baby Boomers will be called upon to un-retire or to stretch their careers, and they too will be the beneficiaries of the tight labor supply. Organizations will convince them to stay or to come back. Money will be one inducement. Passionate work environments will be another. If people find work to be meaningful and joyful, they will be much more likely to stick around. If passion is so critical to individual and organizational success, why isn't it being pursued?

Problems

There are five main reasons why organizations and individuals do not make passionate work a driving force. These are not mutually exclusive and are, in fact, intertwined.

Fear. Living passionately involves taking risks, stretching, and doing new things. Many people are simply afraid of failure. They have either been burned before or dread looking like a failure or silly or stupid to others. Fear causes people to take the safe, secure, nonpassionate route. Over a lifetime this fear builds upon itself, causing once vibrant people to live listlessly and uninspiredly. Fear of rejection causes paralysis, lost opportunities, and often leads to lethargy, bitterness, and depression.

Organizations fear people they can't control. Organizations standardize people. Passionate people are emotional. They cause conflict. They have strong opinions. They have strong desires. They have personal power. Insecure organizations are wary of forceful, independent, intense employees.

Organizations that fear change, fear the marketplace and competition, and fear failure are unlikely to be passionate organizations. Their vision will be safe, their strategic objectives quite reachable, and their leaders tentative.

Lack of Confidence. Related to fear is lack of confidence. When people don't believe in themselves, when they lack self-esteem, and when their self-assessment is poor they are unlikely to be passionate or to do things that lead to passionate work. Instead of applying for that new job because he wants it badly, Joe rationalizes that it wasn't right for him, or that someone with "good connections" is lined up to get it, or any number of blaming tactics to shift responsibility for inaction to someone or something else.

Organizations may lack self-confidence too. They may be timid about starting a new line of business. They may lack courage when tough decisions must be made. Their culture may sustain the status quo. Leadership is an important part of an organization's personality, but it isn't the only part. Each organization has a personality. Those lacking confidence are unlikely to be passionate.

Awareness. Some people are unaware that they are miserable. It often takes a life-changing event—such as the loss of a job, discovering a physical problem, or changing an intimate relationship—for them to reflect on their work. People go through stretches, years even, carrying an underlying, unknown angst that they cannot or do not articulate. Worse, many cannot even describe what they would love to do if they could wave a magic wand and it would become immediately true. "I don't know what to do with my life" is a common lament at any age. Until that question is debated, reviewed, reflected upon, and determined it is mere luck for the person to come across passionate work.

Most organizations don't think in terms of passion. Sports teams do. Advocacy groups do. Many governmental, corporate, and other associations do not. Has your organization assessed what it is passionate about achieving? When was the last time employees jumped up and down and gave high fives because an organizational goal was reached? Big, tough football players do. They cry, they hug, and they whoop it up. Why doesn't yours?

Societal Norms—Reason Versus Emotion. Men aren't supposed to cry, at least, not in public. Men can get angry though. Women who emote are perceived as weak. Society has traditionally frowned on displays of emotion. Though we love a good story about someone who was passionate, our own parents tell us to get the "right" job, even if we don't really like it that much. People are trained to suppress displays of affection. The workplace—for many good reasons—discourages touching, tenderness, and affection among its employees. Society and organizational cultures extol reason, thinking, logic, and analysis.

Many organizations overtly or covertly discourage passion at work. They prefer to live or die by "reason." The mind is all-powerful for these groups, and the heart is of little importance. Organizations have a hard time quantifying "soft" issues and fear what would happen if emotions were unleashed at work. Many organizations are dominated by rationality, the desire for "bottom-line" results, linear thinking, and dispassionate decisionmaking. So what if most new businesses are built on someone's dream, on a major risk, on an intense desire to succeed in helping people, on making a great product or creating something new? Our traditional way of doing business, successful in the past (though it could easily be argued that it has been much less successful than commonly perceived) inhibits us from moving forward to healthier organizational value systems.

People Viewed as "Tools" or "Objects". Much has been written about how people can be perceived as objects. Popular and academic literature has described how men may perceive women as objects. Stories describe how someone was "used" by another person. The objectification of human beings has been roundly criticized from many perspectives.

Some organizations carry an underlying belief that people are things. This is an unstated (usually) conviction that individuals are just input and output systems and that if the right incentive structure and systems are created that they will react like any other well-oiled machine. Machines don't emote, though, do they? Machines are predictable. People are not. We even have predictive maintenance programs and statistical models that predict when machines will fail. We don't know when a person will fall apart or will rise to an occasion.

You can sense when people are viewed as things when they are referred to as "assets" or "intellectual capital" or when leaders talk about throwing "resources" at a problem. These are often useful terms. They indicate the importance of people to an organization, but they also tend to objectify real, live human beings.

When organizations view people as objects it makes sense that they would try to structure emotion out of the system. Organizations want control. When people view themselves as objects—either explicitly or unconsciously—it is unlikely that they will do much more than react to organizational reinforcement schedules like any other rat. When society views people as objects or as parts of societal cogs it makes sense that people are put in their places at early ages and that hopes and dreams and desires are driven out of their suite of acceptable responses to life's opportunities.

Fear, lack of confidence, unawareness, limiting social norms, and holding the view that people are tools or machines all strangle life-giving, passionate work. This book is dedicated to overcoming those individual and organizational limiters.

Overview of Chapters

Transforming Work: The Five Keys to Achieving Trust, Commitment, and Passion in the Workplace is designed to be both informative and useful for individuals and organizations. It contains theoretical grounding and the results of our research but also practical ideas about how to incorporate the concepts into personal and organizational life. This is intended to be a very readable, useful book. We don't want it to simply be a reference or an academic book. It is also a guidebook—something that can actually make a difference in real lives and real organizations.

Chapter 1, "Introduction to Work and Passion," sets the overall context by defining passionate work, illustrating passion through a powerful metaphor, and discussing the importance of passionate work for organizations and individuals. We also discuss the main reasons passionate work is not pursued.

Chapter 2, "The Foundations of Passionate Work," provides the backdrop for our discussion of passionate work. This chapter gives the context for considering how we can apply what we know about passion, intimacy, love, joy, and meaningfulness to our work. This material is intended to enrich our understanding of passion and talks about passion from historical, biological, spiritual, developmental, social/environmental, and psychological perspectives. Concepts that informed our own early perspectives of passionate work, in particular the work of Robert Sternberg, are discussed to give the reader access to information that helped us develop insight into passion and work.

Chapter 3, "The Passion Transformation Process and Cycle," outlines our research and our model. Unlike other research we have conducted in the past, we found the research process itself to be transformational. Participants in our research became emotionally engaged quickly, and the reflective research process we used evoked powerful stories and emotions that enriched us as researchers and as individuals. We have tried to convey a sense of this research journey in Chapter 3. Additionally, we describe the Passion Cycle, the Passion Transformation Model, and the Five Keys to Passionate Work.

Chapter 4, "Occupational Intimacy," explains the term we have coined to describe the outcomes that occur when our models are applied. This chapter gives an in-depth discussion of intimacy and how it applies to work, the barriers to Occupational Intimacy (OI), and the relationship of passionate work to Occupational Intimacy. The interaction of the three elements of OI—nurturing environment, joy or love of work, and meaningfulness—are reviewed and described graphically.

Chapters 5, 6, and 7 give a comprehensive look at the three major processes of the Passion Transformation Model—Discovering, Designing, and Developing. Chapter 5, "Discovering," talks about the goal of discovering, the practices that lead to discovery, and what inhibits discovery. Transformation Theory undergirds the Discovering process and we discuss it in terms of finding passionate work. Chapter 6, using the metaphor of a home, talks about the process of *Designing* a personal journey and work environments that lead to passionate work. This chapter discusses the relationship of passionate work environments to organizational learning. Designing processes that increase the personal agency, motivation, and self-responsibility required to make the transition to passionate work is also part of this discussion. Chapter 7, "Developing," talks about the cycle of Risking, Learning, and Building Self-Efficacy that represents how we put our plans into action. This part of the book describes what risk is and its relationship to learning and self-efficacy. We look here at learning, which is the bedrock of the entire passion transformation process, in the context of its relationship to risk and self-efficacy and, in particular, adulthood. Drawing from Bandura, Knowles, and others' work, we provide conceptual linkages and practical advice about how to apply this to organizational and individual life.

Chapter 8, "Transforming Work," is a call to action. Here we revisit the impact of passion, discuss the value of passionate work to other parts of life, and ask for your commitment. The time to begin living passionately is right now.

EXERCISE ONE: Passionate Work Inventory–Personal

Answer the following questions by choosing a number for each question which best represents how you feel about your current work situation. When you are finished, add up your scores for both sections and, at the bottom, your overall passion for work. This will provide an initial assessment of how you feel about your work today.

Not at all   Some   A great extent

1. To what extent are you willing to
   take risks for things you care about?   1   2   3   4   5   6   7   8

2. To what extent have you discovered
   the kind of work which you can
   be passionate about?   1   2   3   4   5   6   7   8

3. To what extent do you create the right
   conditions to allow you to feel
   passionate about your work?   1   2   3   4   5   6   7   8

4. To what extent do you have
   opportunities for continuous learning
   on your job?   1   2   3   4   5   6   7   8

5. To what extent do you believe you
   have the skills to achieve the things
   you feel passionate about?   1   2   3   4   5   6   7   8

                                                      A _____

26

EXERCISE ONE   (continued)

	Not at all			Some			A great extent	
6. To what extent is your work exciting and not mundane?	1	2	3	4	5	6	7	8
7. To what extent is your work meaningful?	1	2	3	4	5	6	7	8
8. To what extent is your workplace free from manipulation, dishonesty, and lack of trust?	1	2	3	4	5	6	7	8
9. To what extent do you have the freedom to do your job the way you want to do it?	1	2	3	4	5	6	7	8
10. To what extent do you feel that you have the skills, knowledge, and ability to fulfill your work duties?	1	2	3	4	5	6	7	8

B_____

A_____Keys to Passion	B_____Passion Pitfalls	A + B_____Overall Passion
30-40 High	30-40 High	30-40 High
15-29 Average	15-29 Average	30-58 Average
5-14 Low	5-14 Low	10-28 Low

A-Keys to Passion
High	You probably are passionate about your work.
Average	You may need to be more proactive in finding work you are passionate about.
Low	You probably are not doing work that you are passionate about.

B-Passion Pitfalls
High	Your work conditions are conducive for passionate work.
Average	Your work conditions may not be conducive for passionate work.
Low	Your work conditions are not conducive for passionate work.

EXERCISE TWO: Passionate Work Inventory–Organizational

Answer the following questions by choosing a number for each question which best represents how you feel about your organization today. When you are finished, add up your scores and divide your total score by 10. The resulting score will provide an initial assessment of how conducive to passionate work your organization is today.

	Not at all			Some		A great extent		
1. To what extent are employees passionate about their work?	1	2	3	4	5	6	7	8
2. How important is having passionate employees to this organization?	1	2	3	4	5	6	7	8
3. To what extent is the work meaningful for most employees?	1	2	3	4	5	6	7	8
4. To what extent is the work fun for most employees?	1	2	3	4	5	6	7	8
5. To what extent do employees feel that management cares about them as people?	1	2	3	4	5	6	7	8
6. To what extent has the organization spent time and money helping employees develop?	1	2	3	4	5	6	7	8
7. To what extent do managers support existing developmental programs?	1	2	3	4	5	6	7	8
8. To what extent are performance management systems used to develop employees?	1	2	3	4	5	6	7	8
9. To what extent does the organization care about employee attitude and morale?	1	2	3	4	5	6	7	8
10. To what extent is the organization willing to change in order to create a passionate workplace?	1	2	3	4	5	6	7	8

EXERCISE TWO   Passionate Work Inventory–Organizational (continued)

Add up your points. Divide by 10 to get the mean. If your score is:

6-8   Your organization is a Passionate Workplace.

4-5   Your organization needs to work on developing programs for employee development and organizational learning.

1-3   Your organization runs the risk of losing valuable employees or having employees who are just punching the clock.

The Foundations of Passionate Work

The day will come when, after harnessing space, the
    winds, the tides
and gravitation, we shall harness for God the energies of
    love. And on
that day, for the second time in the history of the world,
    we shall
have discovered fire.

—Pierre Teilhard de Chardin

Why Study Love and Passion?

History records countless stories about unrequited love between two people. Management books and periodicals also describe stories of unrequited "love" between organizations and the people who work for them. All too often, an employee joins the organization bursting with anticipation, filled with joy and enthusiasm, but soon realizes that these feelings are not shared by the people working there. Perhaps the employee experiences jealousy or senses fear from other coworkers. Even the boss might be guarded or cynical. Soon the new employee either becomes the living dead himself or leaves the company. How can we avoid this scenario? How can we tap into these emotions rather than tapping them out?

Passion, love, and emotion have been explored throughout history. Philosophy, religion, and psychology have all looked at what happens between two people that causes passion to be kindled, to die, and to reignite. This interest in passion isn't surprising. Strong emotions and commitments play a big part in our lives. But can these feelings be transferred to our work? To organizations? If passion and productivity are related, if creativity is increased when a person is passionate about her work, and if a passionate person inspires other people, then instilling passion in the workplace is key to organizational success.

What can we learn about passion for work from history, biology, and psychology? What is it that attracts one person to another, and why do passionate relationships fail or succeed? How can we apply what we know about passion, intimacy, and commitment to work? How can organizations create passionate work environments using this information? When we began asking ourselves how organizations could cultivate passionate work environments and how individuals could create passion for their work, we started with these seminal questions.

This chapter will discuss the sources of love, passion, intimacy, and commitment. It will provide the underpinnings for both theoretical and practical approaches to creating what we call Occupational Intimacy.

Perspectives on Passion

The Historical Perspective

From earliest recorded history, passion has been a part of the human experience. Fifty-five anonymous love poems exist that date back to around 1300 B.C. Plato said that humans have a variety of emotions such as fear, love, or rage that seek expression. Aristotle used the word "passion" to describe feelings like anger, fear, love, hate, or appetite. He said that individuals who act in harmony with their own nature experience pleasure, whereas those who do not experience pain. Ancient Greeks worshipped two love gods—Aphrodite and Eros. According to Homer, it was Aphrodite toying with Helen that led to the Trojan War. The *Kama Sutra* says, "the stages of the development of passion number ten" (Danielou 1994: 310).

We look at passion and love and their formalized institutions, like marriage, through the eyes of our twenty-first-century experiences and think our beliefs are the only, and the right ways. In fact, however, the ways in which passion and love between individuals have manifested themselves have varied through the ages.

In the fifth century B.C., Athenian marriage was intended to produce children, not to embrace love between husband and wife. Greek myths, however, such as the tragedy of Orpheus and Eurydice, did tell of the passions between woman and man. It was common for Athenian men to have female courtesans or young male lovers, since the practices of the day considered respectable women to be unavailable. Women wishing to be a part of social life often became courtesans, and others turned to relationships with other women.

The Roman Empire was a typical say one thing, practice another society where passion was involved. Espoused Roman values included restraint and monogamy, but prior to marriage young men were allowed to live with mistresses or visit prostitutes. The purpose of marriage was to produce offspring or alliances, not love or passion. The government, through Augustus, imposed strict marriage laws to prevent illegitimate children. Adultery thus became an act against the state instead of mere infidelity. Yet Roman women had time for affairs and, in the midst of this repression, Ovid published *The Art of Love*. This guide to infidelity resulted in his banishment. Though Augustus tried to legislate sexual morality, "he was grappling with a seditious passion so natural for human beings that he was, essentially, warring with nature" (Ackerman 1995: 43).

In the Middle Ages chivalry emerged. Thanks to troubadours, love stories became a part of European literature. "One of the great changes of the Middle Ages was a shift from unilateral to mutual love. That love could be shared, that two people could feel passionate concern and desire for each other, was at first an avant-garde and dangerous idea" (Ackerman 1995: 51). Two people could now feel passion for each other. Instead of love being perceived as vulgar and sinful, troubadours sang of majestic love. The idea of individuals *choosing* to love another, special person was revolutionary at the time. It flew in the face of the traditional, accepted belief that love was only appropriate for God. Personal choice was a new and dangerous idea. Yet lovers of the time spoke of "true love," as something extraordinary and good.

The Renaissance era, like previous times, was disingenuous about love and romance. A duality existed, for example, about how women were viewed. This "was especially glaring during the Renaissance, when women's bodies were depicted as flawless temples of beauty to be studied and worshiped, even as so-called witches were reviled, tortured, and killed in public" (Ackerman 1995: 69). The notion of romance within a marriage, however, began to spread. Shakespeare's plays, like *Romeo and Juliet,* chided arranged marriages that lacked love. His plays involved courtly love. They spoke of romance and of dedication to one true love.

During the Victorian era a prudish attitude reigned publicly. Indecency was considered taboo. Some couples, married for long periods of time, never saw each other without clothes on. On the other hand, it was a time when prostitution, pornography, and perversion flourished. The repressive, puritanical attitude of the time attempted to squelch love and sensuality. These innately human qualities simply converted themselves into other forms.

Through the ages passion has been the stuff of poetry, mythology, moral codes, value systems, and legislation. So much has been written on the topic of emotions that as early as 1734, one author, Charles Lebrun, wrote, "So many learned men have treated of the Passion, that nothing more can be added on the subject . . . " (Strongman [as cited in Freeman 1993: 19]). Yet today passion continues to be a favorite topic of relationship and self-help books. Passion is always a favorite cover-page topic for popular magazines. But even before there was the concept of love, even before passion was captured in love poems hundreds of years before Christ, evolution provided the basic foundations for desire.

The Biological Perspective

> The meeting of two personalities is like the
> contact of two chemical substances;
> if there is any reaction both are transformed.
>
> —CARL JUNG

Aristotle and Plato suggested that emotions have biological roots, but Charles Darwin provided deep insight into how desire and attraction between individuals evolved. Darwin suggested that survival of the species determined the forms of attraction that various species adopted. Darwin's curiosity was provoked when he observed that animals had developed characteristics that weren't necessary for survival. These attributes, he said, might even hinder survivability. He concluded that these features—including, for example, elaborate plumage and antlers—led to the selection of desirable mates and the continuation of a genetic line.

Darwin claimed the selection of mates takes two forms. In one, members of the same sex compete with each other and the winners have greater sexual access to members of the opposite gender. Stronger genes are more likely to be reproduced. In the other form, potential mates are chosen because of specific qualities they display. In this case, particular attraction mechanisms are more likely to be reproduced and genetically continued. In either form of selection, the genetic qualities of mates who are not chosen will be extinguished over time.

Our current, human mating strategies, most of which are subconscious, are the result of centuries of biological selection. The strategies that have survived are ones that have outfought countless others over the years.

In various species, attracting mates can take the form of physical appearance. For humans, physical appearance, or attractiveness, takes the form of stylish clothes, fancy cars, or physical characteristics that are evolutionarily designed to attract mates who will then pass on those characteristics to succeeding generations.

Keeping mates is also an important biological imperative for many species. Those who can keep their mates are more likely to pass on their genes. For ancient women, the need to keep mates was important because they risked losing the resources that a male could provide. Women who were able to keep their mates were also able to pass on those "mate-keeping" genes to offspring. Ancient men who lost their mates risked losing their paternity.

Jealousy is one psychological strategy that evolved to combat infidelity. People who exhibited signs of jealousy and acted to prevent their mate's potential defections had an advantage over those who didn't, and therefore jealousy became an evolutionarily selected trait. Darwin proposed that human emotions are remnants of animal emotions. Darwin felt that emotions are an important part of the biological survival mechanism, and believed that human emotions were essentially biologically based.

Over the ages, evolution has created strong instincts for human beings to be attracted to particular types of individuals. These individuals have desirable abilities that are passed on to succeeding generations. Some attraction mechanisms have been identified through research. Female flirting, the male "chest thrust," the "open smile," and the "copulatory gaze" are all common courting cues. Human beings around the world share many common nonverbal cues. A general pattern to the courting process has even been identified. According to investigators, American singles-bar courting behavior has five distinct stages: (1) the attention-getting stage, (2) the recognition stage, usually when eyes meet eyes, (3) the talk stage, (4) the touching stage, and (5) the total body synchrony stage (Fisher 1992).

Intimacy, a topic that will be covered in more detail in Chapter 4, also has biological roots. Desmond Morris's book, *Intimate Behavior,* is entirely about touching.

> To be intimate means to be close, and I must make it clear at the outset that I am treating this literally. In my terms, then, the act of intimacy occurs whenever two individuals come into bodily contact. It is the nature of this contact, whether it be a handshake or a copulation, a pat on the back or a slap in the face, a manicure or a surgical operation, that this book is about. Something special happens when two people touch one another physically, and it is this something that I have set out to study. (1971: 9)

According to Morris, love is a biological fact. The emotional aspects might be mysterious but the outward, physical signs of loving are easily observed. The strong bonds of attachment between two people are something humans share with thousands of other species, and are not imaginary. Intimacy involves verbal, visual, and olfactory elements "but above all, loving means touching and body contact" (1971: 11). Touching, Morris says, is so basic that it is taken for granted.

If intimacy is touching, as Morris defines it, then is our society becoming less intimate as people withdraw, operate more on the Internet, and create invisible walls around themselves at work and in society? Every person constantly sends out signals that either encourage or discourage intimate contact. It is rare for us to ever touch another person's body unless some accident causes us to touch involuntarily (after which we profusely apologize). In the work environments of today, the question of touching is even more complex. How can individuals and organizations promote intimacy and genuineness without encouraging or endorsing inappropriate invitations to sexual intimacy or touching that is invasive or insensitive to the needs of the individual? Some people simply prefer to be touched less than others do. It's a challenging conundrum.

Not only does passion for another person have biological roots, but it also may be true that we are actually born with a passion for a particular profession or line of work. We are born with temperament, personality traits, brain physiology, and physical characteristics that all have an impact on our personality structure. If that is true, then we would seem to be genetically inclined toward certain kinds of work. Are we indeed natural salespeople or born to be accountants? Lark Roderigues, who paints one-of-a-kind pottery for a living, says she gets up in the morning and does what she loves all day. "I don't feel like I chose this work, I feel like it chose me" ("Business of Bliss" 1999: 21). When we say that a person was made to be a teacher, there is a certain amount of truth to it. We come into the world with a capacity for passion. Sometimes this is manifested in the way a person expresses emotion and love of life. Sometimes it occurs when people find the work they were "born for."

We were "born for" our work in another sense. Spirituality also calls us, or leads us, to the work that we were meant to do.

The Spiritual Perspective

What gives meaning to life? One source of passion is spiritual. The question "Why am I?" has been described as an individual's purpose, mission, vocation, right livelihood, or calling. The question "Why am I?" is at the core of human seeking and therefore has spiritual implications. The word mission comes from the Latin word *missio,* which means "to send." To many Protestant churches, mission means being sent into the world by God to proclaim the Gospel.

In the sense that vocation means being "called," it depends upon hearing a voice that prompts one to live according to an overarching purpose. The word vocation comes from the Latin word *vocatio,* which means summons, and *vocare,* which means to call. This call is to manifest personal gifts and to confirm that one's life is important to the work of the world.

The term vocation was first narrowly defined but has since been more broadly interpreted. Early Christians believed that only a few people were specially and directly called by God. These preachers, prophets, apostles, and other spiritual workers were considered to have an inspired vocation.

Being called to specific work is a key theme in both Jewish and Christian traditions. Moses was sent by God to lead the Israelites out of Egypt (Exodus 3). Abraham was blessed so that the entire earth would be blessed (Genesis 12:2–3). Paul was converted on the road to Damascus to follow Jesus Christ (Acts 9). Paul himself reminded the Ephesians that the gifts Christ gave were "that some would be apostles, some prophets, some evangelists, some pastors and teachers, to equip for the work of ministry . . . " (Ephesians 4: 11–12). Martin Buber (1995), viewing the world from the perspective of Hasidism, believes each person's most important work is to fully develop her or his unique potential and to change the world.

Although the notion of being called to particular life work by an external God is emphasized by the Judeo-Christian tradition, the concept of life purpose itself is much broader. Marsha Sinetar uses the term "right livelihood," which "embodies self-expression, commitment, mindfulness, and conscious choice" (1987: 9–10). The term right livelihood comes from the Buddhist tradition, which defines it as "work consciously chosen, done with full awareness and care, and leading to enlightenment" (9).

The Hindu concept of "dharma" is "the assignment to each man of a place within the world order which he must fulfill in order to have a higher chance in another life" (Erikson 1969: 79). Gandhi himself often acted upon his "inner voice," which would unexpectedly speak to him and then insist on his commitment (1969: 412).

Zen Buddhist beliefs recognize the uniqueness of each person and the importance of becoming. Zen master Suzuki said, "Each one of us must make his own true way, and when we do, that way will express the universal way" (1994: 111).

Having a deep sense of purpose and meaning gives passion to life. Are there also particular times in our lives when we are more likely to search for passion and purpose?

Development Theories and Passion

Are there different stages in life when passion is more likely to develop or emerge? If passion is related to meaning or mission or purpose in life, then developmental theorists have provided some possible areas of exploration. Development theorists have touched on the relationship of mission, or purpose in life, to adult development. Roger Gould describes the development of "life dreams" (1978: 78) as adults grow. Life dreams constructed around parental expectations, ideal role models, or overcompensation for emotional insecurities can result in unhappiness unless the individual can "take responsibility for his own adult dream . . . " (85). Instead of remaining locked into the past, Gould says, "we have to win internal permission to be what we find ourselves becoming" (84).

The formation and modification of a dream is included in Levinson's developmental theory as well. Levinson believes that one of the major tasks of what he calls the Novice Phase is to form a "Dream" (1978: 91) and to live it out. This phase runs from around age seventeen through about age thirty-three. The Dream is the kind of life one wants to lead as an adult. It has the quality of a vision. It represents something to be strived for, such as the role of an imagined hero, or even the more realistic but still inspiring role of craftsperson, parent, or community leader. This Dream is at first amorphous. The task of a person in this phase is to further define it and to determine the ways to live it.

Sherrill says that the meaning of life can be viewed symbolically as a treadmill, a saga, or a pilgrimage. The treadmill represents a feeling that life has no meaning. Sherrill says this view is experienced by millions and has the "peculiar quality of drying up the souls of the myriads of little people who carry [modern] civilization on their backs" (1951: 4).

The saga is a life of heroism, as the individual traverses and survives hardships and challenges to arrive at her own end. The saga teaches and honors secular virtues like courage, patience, endurance, and self-sacrifice. This view of life recognizes and celebrates the human qualities that exist within the treadmill itself.

A pilgrim is someone who refuses to walk the treadmill at all. She denies that existence and takes instead a journey or quest. This is a journey of the mind, and even those pilgrims at heart who cannot physically journey forth can deny the treadmill and live a life of pilgrimage.

The model proposed by Belenky, Clinchy, Goldberger, and Tarule provides yet another potential perspective of passion development. The metaphor they uncovered through their interviews with women was that of "gaining a voice" (1986: 16). This metaphor was originally proposed by Carol Gilligan in her seminal work, *In a Different Voice* (1982). Gaining a voice came to be understood by the researchers as the interconnected development of mind, voice, and self. It was the link between the five perspectives of "knowing" they identified, which represent the development of progressive personal agency. These five perspectives are silence, received knowledge, subjective knowledge, procedural knowledge, and constructed knowledge.

Cochran views vocation itself as a developmental process. To Cochran, vocation is "the elevated sense of a life's calling" (1990: 2). Not everyone has a vocation, he says, which gives special status and has great value. Vocation is the unity of person and life's work, and they cannot be separated.

Each of the developmental theories described above has embedded within itself the concept of passion for one's life work. This notion may be called a life dream, the Dream, an identity crisis, voice, or phases of vocation, but it appears to be integral to human growth.

Given the things we have no control over, our genetic code and our natural developmental processes, it is interesting to look at an area where we initially have a limited control that increases as we move into adulthood—our environment.

Social/Environmental

What society expects of a young woman or man from specific economic, geographical, or educational backgrounds is often embedded within the individual self. His or her "Why am I?" tends to be objectified through a social role—for example, mother, father, son of a doctor, daughter of an inventor, Baptist, or Socialist. Society expects a person from a particular background to act in certain roles and in socially accepted vocations.

Alarmingly, many people at a very young age have already limited their career expectations because they have adopted from their environment assumptions about what they can or cannot do. Potential lines of work that would be natural sources of passion are eliminated before the person even has a chance to try them out.

At early ages children receive messages—positive or negative—from parents and later peers, teachers, and coaches that either encourage or discourage the pursuit of passionate activities. At an early age a child may be conditioned to believe she or he does not have the talent or the character to achieve particular dreams. Early environmental conditions often constrain people from following their passion for a lifetime.

Later environmental influences can be just as deadly. It is difficult for a person to think outside of a particular career, vocation, profession, or craft once she has been indoctrinated by school, orientation, value or reward systems, or other forms of norming. Lawyers become part of the "club." Union members become part of the "brotherhood." Members of the military are "the few, the proud, the Marines," or for the U.S. Navy, it's "Not just a job, it's an adventure." In the U.S Air Force men and women are told to "Aim High," and in the U.S. Army young soldiers are told that they are going to be all that they can be. Organizations, often with good intentions and for good reasons, socialize employees into their cultures. This process can be quite constraining. People often accept outcomes that they don't have to accept simply because they have been conditioned to believe that their options are limited, or because they have given up looking for alternatives. Leider and Shapiro ask the question, "Are you wasting your natural talents because your career chose you, rather than you choosing it carefully?" (1995: 74). They point out that many people don't know what they want to be early in life. By the time they figure it out, they think it's too late to pursue their dream. Some people never figure it out. The external environment not only tends to cause people to limit their thinking about what they would really love to do but also limits their perceived sense of personal power.

We know there are biological, environmental, spiritual, and developmental foundations for passion. The source that seems to garner the most popular attention is psychological, perhaps because it relates so closely to our interpersonal relationships. The topic mostly clearly related to passionate relationships is love.

Psychological Theories of Love and Attachment

We were deeply influenced in our thinking about passionate work by the theoretical and practical discussions of passionate love between two people that are found in the literature. We asked ourselves if it were possible to apply what we knew about passionate love to passionate work. Our research shows that the two are analagous. One person who has written very insightfully about love is Sternberg.

Sternberg's Triangle of Love

Robert Sternberg starts his book, *The Triangle of Love,* by saying that "Love is one of the most intense and desirable of human emotions. People may lie, cheat, steal, and even kill in its name—and wish to die when they lose it. Love can overwhelm anyone at any age" (1987: 3).

Sternberg put forth a theory of love and relationship using a triangle as a metaphor to describe the way key elements interact to create love. Three ingredients are included in Sternberg's triangle of love: Passion, Intimacy, and Decision/Commitment.

Intimacy, to Sternberg, refers to feelings of closeness, bondedness, and connectedness. Intimacy is composed of a number of elements, which include:

1. Desiring to promote the welfare of the loved one.
2. Experiencing happiness with the loved one.
3. Holding the loved one in high regard.
4. Being able to count on the loved one in times of need.
5. Having mutual understanding with the loved one.
6. Sharing oneself and one's possessions with the loved one.
7. Receiving emotional support from the loved one.
8. Giving emotional support to the loved one.
9. Communicating intimately with the loved one.
10. Valuing the loved one. (1987: 38–40)

Intimacy results from frequent interconnections between people, and intimate couples have strong ties between each other. Self-disclosure is probably the starting place for intimacy to develop. "It is well known that self-disclosure begets self-disclosure; if you want to get to know what someone is like, let him or her learn about you" (41). Until the walls that separate one from another are broken down there can be no intimacy, and until one person is willing to be vulnerable, the other person is unlikely to do so. Intimacy develops over time and can be difficult to achieve. Once attained it is difficult to maintain because of the threat of self-disclosure but also because of the danger of losing one's identity when consumed by a relationship. Sternberg says, "The result is a balancing act between intimacy and autonomy which goes on throughout the lives of most couples . . . " (1987: 41).

Passion is Sternberg's second foundation of love. Passion is "the expression of desires and needs" (1987: 42), which he describes as self-esteem, sexual fulfillment, nurturance, affiliation, dominance, and submission. Passion interacts with intimacy—where passion might pull the couple together in the first place, intimacy helps to maintain the closeness of the relationship over time. Though the term passion is often used interchangeably with sex, passion is not always sexual. Any kind of psychophysiological arousal can generate passion, including meeting the need to affiliate, to dominate, or for submission.

Interestingly, passion is reinforced when what is desired is not always obtained. In other words, part of the quality of passion has to do with the desire for something. If a person always achieves his or her desires, then desire fades. Alternatively, if a person never is rewarded, then he or she will probably give up. "Passion thrives on the intermittent reinforcement that is intense at least in the early stages of a relationship" (Sternberg 1987: 45).

Decision and commitment are two aspects that represent the third foundation of Sternberg's triangle of love. Decision is the short-term conclusion to love another person. Commitment is the longer-term aspect of maintaining that love. Simply deciding to love does not necessarily mean that it will last. Marriage is the legal, explicit commitment to the decision to love the other person for life.

When passion and intimacy invariably wax and wane, it is the decision/commitment aspect of a relationship that keeps it together. It is indispensable for getting through the waning times in order to return to the better, waxing times.

These three components of love—intimacy, passion, and decision/commitment—interact with each other. Intimacy and commitment are usually more stable in close relationships than passion, which may vary. In short-term involvements, passion tends to play a large part, intimacy perhaps much less of a part, and decision/commitment no part at all. In longer-term, close relationships, intimacy and decision/commitment play much larger parts and passion may play a lesser part, which may decline over time.

Sternberg describes the interrelationships between the three components. For example, "liking" describes a relationship with only the component of intimacy. "Infatuated love" describes a relationship with only passion. A relationship with only decision/commitment is "empty love." Intimacy plus passion equals "romantic love," intimacy plus commitment "companionate love," and passion plus commitment is what Sternberg calls "fatuous love." Complete love, which includes all three elements—passion, intimacy, and decision/commitment—is "consummate love." Consummate love is the ultimate. Attaining consummate love is no guarantee it will last. "Consummate love, like other things of value," Sternberg says, "must be guarded carefully" (60), and a couple or a person may not even be aware that it is lost until long after it is gone.

TABLE 2.1   Sternberg's Taxonomy of Kinds of Love

Kind of Love	Intimacy	Passion	Decision/ Commitment
Nonlove	-	-	-
Liking	+	-	-
Infatuated Love	-	+	-
Empty Love	-	-	+
Romantic Love	+	+	-
Compassionate Love	+	-	+
Fatuous Love	-	+	+
Consummate Love	+	+	+

NOTE: + = component present; - = component absent. These kinds of love represent idealized cases based on the triangular theory. Most loving relationships will fit between categories, because the components of love occur in varying degrees, rather than being simply present or absent.

SOURCE: Sternberg 1987: 51.

Relationships of any type, Sternberg says, "are constructions that decay over time if they are not maintained and even improved. A relationship cannot take care of itself, any more than a building can. Rather, we must take responsibility for making our relationships the best they can be and constantly work to understand, build, and rebuild them" (83).

Sternberg's concepts will be discussed in more detail in Chapter 4, where we relate them to our concept of Occupational Intimacy.

Attraction and Attachment

In many ways we are attracted to people whose presence rewards us. We may be attracted to a person because we enjoy his company or because she encourages or praises us. "Equity theory implies that over the long term, it is important that both members of a couple feel that their rewards and punishments from the relationship are approximately equal. What starts to destroy a relationship, is when it is always the same person making the sacrifices" (Sternberg 1987: 120).

Studies have shown that people living closely together are more likely to become friends than those living farther apart, and people who interact more frequently are more likely to experience increased attraction. The easier it is to interact, the easier it is to develop relationships. Likewise, lack of closeness can make it more difficult to maintain attraction to another person (Brehm 1992).

Physical attractiveness, especially in initial meetings, also increases actual attraction. Why? In addition to natural, physical attraction, people tend to generalize, believing that a physically attractive person is probably also personally attractive and is more likely to be successful in life. We may perceive the beautiful as more talented or having more social skills. Finally, people may be attracted to individuals perceived as good-looking because of the positive social effects of being associated with such people.

We are also often attracted to people who are similar to us in a variety of ways that include personality, socioeconomic history, or their beliefs. Sometimes people are attracted, however, to people who are different or complementary. Sometimes people are attracted to others whose behavior complements their own (shy-assertive, for example). The ability to share resources has also traditionally been a source of attraction.

Sometimes attraction to another person is increased because there are obstacles in the way. Although it seems counterintuitive, passion is often reduced over time when obstacles are taken away and the relationship becomes easier. Alternatively, desire for another person is often increased when, for whatever reason, that person is hard to get.

Summary

Think of everything you have ever imagined about passion. Think back to your own experiences with passion, personally and professionally. The day the CEO told the whole management group that you were the reason earnings were exceptional this year. The morning you got to work and found out that you'd been transferred to the job you'd coveted. The meeting when one of your employees told you what an inspiration you'd been to him. The night you came home to your family and told them that you'd been picked to lead the new product development team. How did you feel? What did you think? Did your heart pound and your body sweat? Did you say a prayer or feel a blessing? Did your coworkers make you feel special? Those emotions, thoughts, physical reactions, surrounding environment, and that connection to the spirit are the sources of passion.

Passion, or love, between two people was the starting point of our search for passionate work. In this chapter we have glimpsed how passion has been perceived through the centuries, looked at how our biological roots are the wellspring of passion, touched on the spiritual sources of passion, thought about the developmental aspects of passion, and looked at the psychology of passion. Now it is time to turn to our research and to a more specific understanding of the relationship of passion to our work.

Development of the Passion Transformation Model

The Passion Transformation Model originated from the biological, social, environmental, and psychological foundations of passion and love as discussed above. It is also anchored in other theoretical concepts, such as transformational learning theory, which will be discussed in later chapters. Chapter 3 will discuss our research and describe the model in detail. Subsequent chapters will cover the practical implications for creating personal and organizational passion.

EXERCISE THREE: **Foundations of Passion Questionnaire**

This book focuses on passion for work. We know, however, that the potential for passion permeates our lives. Every person has the capacity for passion—with others, with work, for causes, for personal growth, and so on. Before we dive into the relationship of passion to work, take some time to reflect generally on yourself as a passionate person.

Do you think of yourself as a passionate person? Why or why not? How would others answer this question about you, and why?

Describe the things you are passionate about and why you feel that way about them. What or who do you really care about?

Are there situations where you have lost your passion for life or parts of your life? What happened? Why?

What sources of passion are most important to you? Spiritual? Biological? Interpersonal or social? Others?

There are many ways to experience and to express passion for something or someone. How do you do it? How would you like to do it?

What areas in your life lack passion? Why? Is that okay, or are you missing something?

What do you do to create passion for yourself? What works and what doesn't?

Summarize your passion for life today.

Passion Transformation Process and Cycle

Organizational, educational, and clinical psychologists have long studied motivation. There have been many different theories put forth to describe how to develop motivation within individuals, organizations, and systems. Despite a host of papers and books on the subject, motivation continues to be a national concern. Good employees burn out, motivation turns to apathy, and there is a continual brain drain from organizations. As we stated in Chapter 1, the workplace of the future is going to be very different in how we recruit, develop, and keep employees. Demographic researchers of Generation X paint a picture that includes sign-up bonuses, little company loyalty, and severe shortages of trained technical employees in the coming years. Motivating employees will be key to keeping good people from leaving. Many companies already face these problems.

In examining motivation theories, there appears to be a lack of emphasis on the emotional impact of work. Various models look at equity, valence, work environment, hygiene factors, and empowerment issues, all of which are important. However, since work is where most people spend the majority of their waking hours, it makes sense that the factors that make us human are important at work. The basis of our model for developing and maintaining motivation for work is drawn from the research in the psychological field of passion. The development of our model began with a search for what makes people love their work. What makes a passionate employee? Why do passionate employees lose their passion?

Passion has been studied in the literature, usually in the area of relationships and love. We borrowed the concepts from this research but instead of looking at relational love, we looked at love of work. We started with Sternberg's 1987 seminal work, *The Triangle of Love,* where he dissected the components of love and viewed passion as playing a key role in emotional attachment and intimacy. This led to our thinking about the role of intimacy in work. If intimacy fuels passion, then how can we become "intimate" or close to our work? What is "occupational intimacy"? How can organizations foster this concept?

The purpose of this chapter is to present our Passion Transformation Model and the research that led to its development. The model is based on the results of a qualitative research study influenced by several key theories in the areas of passion, learning, and intimate relationships.

Learning from Adult Lives

We adopted a perspective that people create meaning within lived experiences from which information and interpretation can be drawn (Watkins, Marsick, Honold, and O'Neil 2000). The data gathered were subjective and based on over 300 critical incidents and interviews.

Qualitative research is experiencing a growing influence within the social sciences. This growth follows the proliferation of quantitative, empirical research that dominated the early to late twentieth century. Qualitative methods emerged because empirical methods could not answer many questions about the human condition. Social scientists, trained almost exclusively in quantitative methods, tried valiantly to measure human emotions, behaviors, and individualities. Much of this research yielded bits and pieces, but not the bigger picture, of human nature. "Common sense tells us that the minds and behaviors of human beings are not like the elements of the earth or other easily dissected objects. People's behaviors and attitudes can, and perhaps should, be studied in other than empirical ways" (Bleyl 2000).

Traditionally, motivation in the workplace has also been studied empirically. Motivation has been seen as an instinctual drive, a learned response, a personality trait, a social phenomena, and as a cognitive attribution or construct. Major theories of motivation have centered on different kinds of drives, needs, equity issues, and personal response patterns. Yet with all we know about motivation, people still work in jobs they dislike and organizations find it difficult to keep motivated individuals.

Our approach has been to take a different route to understanding motivation and passion. Our study is grounded in a humanist approach. We believe that it is through the actual human experience that answers to these important questions can be derived.

The human experience has always been told through stories. These stories began with cave drawings, Egyptian hieroglyphics, and ancient documents such as the Dead Sea Scrolls, and continue today through our more modern personal journals kept on laptops. Stories inform our values, principles, desires, and heritage. Analyzing stories is best done by looking at them as a gestalt——at how the stories tell us more than just the words put together. To empirically analyze a person's story would be like trying to describe a beautiful impressionistic painting by describing each dab of color.

The Importance of Stories

If we are to understand an aspect of human nature, what better place to study it than from the perspective of humans themselves? Robert Coles, in *The Call of Stories: Teaching and the Moral Imagination* talks about how important stories have been to developing his knowledge and understanding of the world. He found that through stories, he could fully enter another's life. His father said to him "that novels contained 'reservoirs of wisdom,' out of which he and our mother were drinking" (1989: xii).

Adult biographies are now being used more often to help individuals understand their own lives, to gain insights about themselves, and to help us understand human nature. They provide what is called *clinical knowledge* as opposed to scientific knowledge (Dominice 2000). "In contrast to scientific knowledge, clinical knowledge arises out of collaborative analysis of single cases that are considered meaningful. It corresponds to a theoretical look at critical situations from within" (12). As opposed to analytical, linear types of analyses that tell us *what* is happening, narratives give us an understanding of *how* and *why* things happen.

In our research we asked over 300 working adults to share critical incidents regarding their experiences with passion and work. We asked them to tell us about a time they were passionate about their work, what created that passion, how they maintained it, and if they lost it, why, and how they got it back. These were written narratives and short interviews. We also conducted seven in-depth interviews with people who had been recommended as being very passionate about their work. We have stories from both men and women, ages eighteen to over sixty. The occupations of these individuals were quite diverse. They ranged from educators to retail sales people to medical doctors to government employees.

When we could, we brought interviewees together so they could describe their stories to one another. When the groups listened to these stories, incredible emotions were evident. These stories triggered new insights for both the participants and the researchers.

One semester, in a graduate Adult Learning class, the students were asked to give a brief overview of their critical incidents. We had two and a half hours to cover twenty students' remarks. The first few stories had such an impact on the other students that we had to extend these feedback sessions for two more class periods, a total of seven and a half hours. We could have gone on much longer. There were enumerable questions and dialogue on similar experiences and emotions that the stories uncovered for all the students. As college professors, this was one of our most impactful semesters. In fact, students still, several semesters later, come to talk to us about that experience.

Understanding the Stories

The task of interpreting individuals' stories can be daunting. Since stories belong to the world of meaning and reflection, the accuracy of reliable data does not exist. Asking for stories opens the door to imaginative interpretations of one's life events. So how does one go about analyzing such data?

We went through a process of content analysis but were reminded that content analysis doesn't give undeniable truth; instead, the "truth" is found in the context and personality of the individual's particular story. You can't understand specific findings without the context and descriptive narration of the story. To preserve the validity and integrity of these narratives we had to take particular care in their analysis. We not only discussed them ourselves, working to come to an understanding of what was actually being said, but we also asked other researchers trained in qualitative methods to do independent analyses. From this careful, iterative work, we were able to delve deeply into our interviewees' understanding of passion and its relationship to their work.

A Ph.D. student in health education told us this story. It is an example of how one person pursued her passion.

> My decision to return to school was based on many factors. By returning full-time I hoped to complete my undergraduate degree within two years. During this transition I had to make many decisions. . . . Because I was weighted down by tradition, I sought only to complete my undergraduate degree. I was able to capitalize on the energy that allowed me to work 40+ hours per week and exchanged that for energy and passion to pursue my studies. . . . My passion also allowed me to discover that I could achieve in an academic environment. . . . Much to my surprise, my drive and passion also yielded a scholarship for returning women students . . . I took the responsibility of directing my life instead of depending on others and learning how to operate in a less structured environment. . . . Not only was passion involved but considerable development had also emerged.

The analyses of these narratives uncovered several barriers to achieving and sustaining passion for work. The stories often described very painful experiences. People talked about manipulative managers, feelings of personal failure, or distressing and depressing work environments. The barriers to passionate work also included boring or routine work, working in an overly controlled environment, feeling inadequate, and working under conditions of dishonesty or lack of trust.

The stories also spoke of how passion ebbs and flows. There was a traceable, repetitive pattern. Individuals wrote about having great passion and that after a while, when the job was no longer interesting, they had to find a new passion. In the stories they talked about losing their way and not knowing how to find new passions time and time again. In examining this cycle we discovered what helped someone to find a new passion. And it was always the same—learning something new.

Learning, in their stories, was central to finding, keeping, and retaining passion. Learning was the intervention that turned people from becoming the living dead to feeling alive and vital. Whether learning was imposed on someone or arose naturally within the individual, it was the crucial process related to passionate work.

Another significant finding was the source of passion within individuals. Where does passion come from within someone? What sparks us, motivates us, turns the faucet on? Four sources of passion have been found and documented in the literature (Freeman 1993): cognitive, emotional, physiological, and environmental. Our study found the same four sources of passion, as well as an additional source—spirituality. Many of our interviewees felt very strongly that their spirituality was a strong source of the passion within them.

Most important, these stories provided rich descriptions of how people find and keep their passion for work. They provided real-life examples of processes and strategies for developing and maintaining passionate work. These processes fell into five areas we have labeled as the keys to helping individuals who have lost their way or who find their passion waning to regain a love for work. The findings from this study show that passion, self-knowledge, the work environment, learning, and productivity are related. People with passion for their work are more likely to work harder and more creatively.

As individuals, we need to be aware of how to help ourselves when faced with passionless work. Organizations need to understand the forces that can affect the passions of employees. The results from our research and the concepts we borrowed from various theoretical sources provided the basis for our Passion Transformation Model.

Our Results

Passion Pitfalls

When passion doesn't exist or when it fades, we become frustrated, apathetic, or detached. Work just isn't any fun. When people are dispassionate, the organization begins to atrophy because good employees leave and the organization is left with deadwood——those who can't regain their passion. Understanding the conditions that cause passions to die is vital to facilitate both individual and organizational change. We have discovered four common pitfalls, ways in which people fall into the pit of passionless work.

Pitfall #1—Boring or Meaningless Work. When you walk, day after day, into work that you find boring, it's time to change. One person we talked to called it "the exotic becoming mundane." If you can't change jobs immediately, at least find ways to make it interesting or different. A director of economic development for a large company told us that her job "doesn't change that much year-to-year; the faces change, the names change, but what you do is a little bit the same. The way I keep going is to find some sort of new projects—things that help me learn and try to do something different." She says that what she's found out about herself is that she likes ". . . sort of dreaming up the idea and rallying up the people to do it, to make this thing happen and once it starts to happen then I've lost interest." So she makes sure that her job includes opportunities to work on projects that are interesting and new.

Pitfall #2—Working in an Overly Controlled Setting. Described as "exhausting to deal with," work situations that limit your initiative, creativity, and the ability to make decisions are very defeating. A woman manager told us,

> The fellow I reported to had an extremely outrageous need to control everybody. As long as you were doing exactly what he thought you should be doing, exactly the way he thought you should be doing it, you didn't bump into the problem. But the minute you wanted to take off and take it somewhere, or broaden it, or do something different with it, then he thought—it was horrid, what happened. No matter how hard I worked to have passion, being controlled and manipulated and punished for going outside of some boundaries, [destroyed my passion].

"The field of plastic surgery always was exciting and challenging," a retired physician told us. "The ability to help others was quite rewarding until managed care came into play and we lost our ability to make decisions. It became a frustrating task!" Another woman said,

> I was working in a support position to a director for a program I passionately believed in. I was given room to create new programs and strengthen present ones. My passion was in fine shape until I began to be treated dif-

ferently by my Director. She began giving me fewer responsibilities, she took credit for my ideas, and she stopped giving me evaluations. She became less and less available and unwilling to discuss the problem. It became unbearable. All I could think of was "How do I get out of here?"

If you constantly feel stifled, it's time to talk to the boss . . . or move on.

Pitfall #3—Feeling Inadequate. Continuous growth and stretching yourself are important qualities of passionate people, but when we feel inadequate or feel like failures or are constantly discouraged, we are in a situation that decreases passion. We feel scared. We are unwilling to take a risk. A college professor who became a university administrator told us,

> I was in over my head and I hated it. One of the reasons that I would lose my passion is if I was doing something I felt I was not good at, and that really killed me. That I just felt that I wasn't doing it well, that I was letting people down. I was letting myself down and I wasn't following through on things I should have and I let them just sit. You're never supposed to let a piece of paper go by you. I had pieces of paper going by me twelve times, and I still didn't do anything about it. So I really was out of my element to say the least.

Feelings of inadequacy, of not being able to hold your own, makes people lose their passion. Organizations that do not provide adequate training may contribute to passionless employees.

Pitfall #4—Manipulation, Dishonesty, Lack of Trust. We heard story after story describing deceptive bosses or work situations that destroy passion. Working in this kind of atmosphere is deadly. Several of our interviewees told stories about coming up with new projects and ideas and having them literally stolen by their superiors. One woman said, "My creative ideas and courses were claimed by my boss as his. I felt very betrayed, stabbed in the back, and unwilling to trust the person who took the trust away." A thirty-seven-year-old male operations support manager told us, "Before I could introduce my ideas, my immediate supervisor took some of my ideas and created his own program. He brought his program to senior staff and got an approved budget and a substantial bonus check. I lost my passion and took another position." No one thrives in an environment that lacks trust.

The Passion Cycle

When asked about factors affecting the increase or decrease of passion for work we found data that closely resembles the cycle of passion in relationships. In 1999, Baumeister and Bratslavsky found that intimate relationships tend to follow a cyclical pattern. This pattern indicated that in the initial phase of a relationship, when couples are learning much about each other, passion increases until it reaches a peak and then slowly begins to decrease. They found that if new learning did not take place, passion would die.

This pattern is also suggested in Fisher's (1992) *Anatomy of Love.* She chronicles the biological basis of mating behavior and intimate relationships. She found that passion for humans, after approximately four years, tends to fade if couples do not have an interruption or change in their relationship, such as the birth of a child. This four-year cycle tends to cor-

FIGURE 3.1   The Cycle of Intimacy

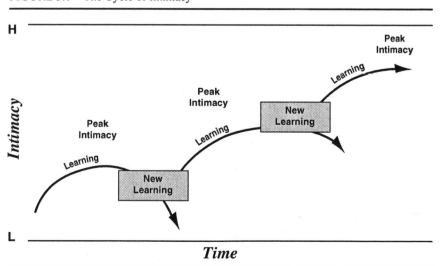

SOURCE: Adapted from Baumeister & Bratslavsky 1999.

FIGURE 3.2   The Passion Cycle

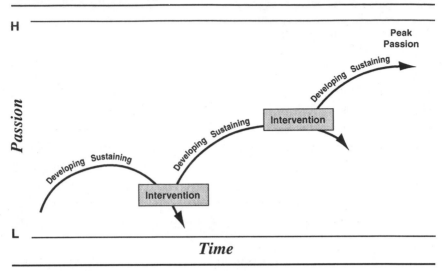

relate with the time necessary to have and raise an infant. Thus, the fading of passion would occur about the time a child is three years old.

In our study we found a similar pattern for passionate work. Our subjects described when passion occurs—usually at the start of a job or a new project. Passion for work tends to fade and then die away when employees experience one or more of the passion pitfalls described above. Our interviewees talked about the initial learning phase, when passion began to develop. As learning increased, so did their passion for work. Passion tends to plateau for a period of time when one feels skilled at work. If the work becomes boring or they experience any of the passion pitfalls, then passion declines, sometimes very rapidly. The individuals who were able to regain passion had looked around for their next challenge, as soon as they realized they were in a plateau period or in decline. Some people did this consciously, whereas others seemed to have a pattern, perhaps unconscious, where they pursued new interests as prior interests faded.

Three different patterns were reported by our subjects. The first is Passion Extinction. This is characterized by a sharp increase in passion when the learning curve is greatest. Then, when an employee learns his or her job and it no longer offers any challenge, new learning, or growth, passion begins to die. We have all known people who have given up and resigned themselves to boring and passionless work. These are the dead-

FIGURE 3.3 Passion Patterns

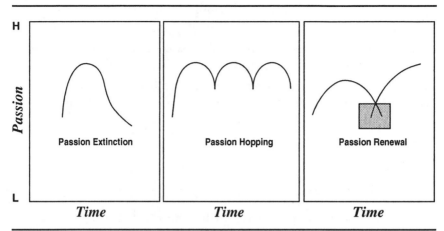

wood in organizations. We refer to them as the living dead. Usually they are longtime employees who for one reason or another have given up on trying to find excitement or challenge in their work. All they have to look forward to is retirement. Their attitudes are poor, their work is below standard, and they can be the proverbial "rotten apples" that spoil the others.

A second pattern is that of Passion Hopping. This person tends to jump ship when his or her job becomes routine. Rather than investing the energy to take on new challenges or to ask for greater responsibilities, this person looks either outside the organization for a new job or applies for other positions within the organization. This pattern is tied to supply and demand. When demand is high and the supply of available personnel is low, it is easier to move than to stay. With the expected changes on the horizon for the number of available employees, we are going to find more people who passion hop rather than stay in their positions. Also, such individuals are not willing to invest the time to develop strong ties to an organization, so they just move on.

The last pattern, that of Passion Renewal, is more closely aligned with the goal of our model. In this pattern, individuals reported that as passion began to fade, they found themselves asking hard questions, such as, "What do I really want to do? What can make staying in this job worthwhile?" These individuals said that they do not let themselves become bored or without passion for their work.

We asked people what they did to regain their passion. Most responded that they took on new learning, a new job, redesigned their own jobs, or found something in their life outside of work to sustain them. Some of our respondents didn't realize that it was a conscious choice to always strive to keep their passion. They just did it naturally. We found that passion can be renewed in a job if the learning process begins again, for example, by switching jobs, taking on a new project, or being given added responsibilities. As passion begins to wane, an intervention is necessary.

Learning Organisms

This cycle demonstrates the necessity to continually learn and develop. We need to make our world interesting and stimulating. What one finds interesting and stimulating will differ from person to person; but the fact remains that it is the same issue for everyone. We are learning organisms, making us lifelong learners.

We know that the greatest amount of learning occurs between the ages of birth to five years of age. During this time children learn to walk, talk, operate, and find their place in the world. Learning continues at a high rate after that through schools, churches, families, and peers. But learning doesn't stop when we finish school. In fact, learning never stops. As adults, we are still continually learning. It usually doesn't occur in formal settings, but nevertheless, it continues. We are bombarded constantly by the media, which throws information at us to buy, sell, or change ourselves. At work we have to learn our jobs, new processes, and new technologies. At home, we learn to live with a significant other, to raise children, and to patch the roof over our head. Socially, we learn to be citizens who vote, help others, and make the world a safe place to live.

In 1984, Elliot Aronson wrote a book called *The Social Animal.* His opening quote is from Aristotle, who said,

Man is by nature a social animal; an individual who is unsocial naturally and not accidentally is either beneath our notice or more than human. Society is something in nature that precedes the individual. Anyone who either cannot lead the common life or is so self-sufficient as not to need to, and therefore does not partake of society, is either a beast or a god. (*Politics*, c. 328 B.C., xviii)

To live socially one must be able to learn. Thus, it is learning that precedes socialization, just as it is the means to that end. Therefore, by virtue of being learning organisms, men and women become social animals.

If you have ever witnessed the first time a baby makes a mobile move by kicking it, you know the look of pure happiness. Or the agony and then joy when you finally learn to ride a bike. We are happiest when we are learning. When we are learning all about that wonderful person we are falling in love with, when we are learning how to do our job competently or when we are learning about our favorite hobby—that is when we are happy and passionate.

People who continue to have positive learning experiences at work are passionate about what they do. But too often we have lifeless workforces who engage in hobbies, outside interests, and even turn to illicit activities to add some stimulation to an otherwise mundane existence. Organizations and employers need to understand this basic drive for learning and growth. If your employees don't find your workplace interesting and stimulating, they will pour their energies somewhere else. Organizations need to try to harness this latent passion that exists in everyone.

Our Passion Transformation Model serves as the intervention needed when passion begins to fade during this cycle. This model begins and ends with learning as its foundation and provides processes to continually feed passion.

Passion Transformation Model

Our model for discovering, designing, and developing passion for work is the intervention we prescribe for helping people find or renew their passion. We outlined the importance of having such a process available to employees in Chapter 1. In tomorrow's workplace, employers will have to have programs and processes in place to continually attract and keep good employees. Our model is based on the relevant theories underlying passion and we have found evidence to support it in the stories working adults have related to us. Our model relates the sources under-lying passion as inputs to a systematic process of Discovering, Design-ing, and Developing, with the output resulting in greater passion and what we define as Occupational Intimacy. This same process can be used to develop passion for work, for relationships, or for life in general. Within the Discovering, Designing, and Developing processes are en-ablers that promote each process. The enablers and the overriding pro-cesses of Discovering, Designing, and Developing can be intertwined and repeated as necessary. Chapters 5, 6 and 7 will each respectively cover the three major components of the model.

The Passion Transformation Model is comprised of the sources un-derlying passion and a transformational cycle that includes three dis-tinct growth processes that lead to passion or renewed passion. The growth processes are iterative and both individuals and organizations can use them. Individuals can use them to develop personal passion and organizations can use them to design programs and practices for mak-ing the workplace more supportive of passionate employees. This devel-opmental, transformational model, if used by either individuals or organizations, can help to sustain the energy and interest of employees in the workplace.

Sources

Several factors influence our level of passion. Some are outside our con-trol. For example, each person is born with a certain capacity for pas-sion. Each person comes into the world with biological mechanisms that drive him or her. From our parents and grandparents we inherit a range of predispositions—including fight or flight instincts, the drive to sur-vive, and emotional tendencies. We are also powerfully affected by the first few years of our life. Changing the qualities that our parents and early environment foist on us is difficult. We also can't control luck—whether or not we find the right job at the right time or the right person in the right place is often outside our control.

Beyond these limiting factors, we have an incredible opportunity to make our lives passionate ones. The ability to make choices that lead to the kind of lives we can pursue with enthusiasm and energy is within our power, as well as the ability to discover the kind of work that we can

FIGURE 3.4   The Passion Transformation Model

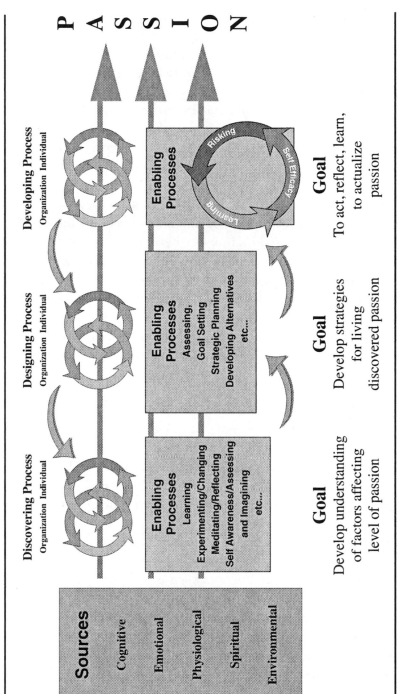

follow with passion. Also within our power is the discipline and determination to then create the life we imagine and yearn for. After taking into consideration the things that we cannot change, the rest is entirely up to us. To a large extent if we want to have an exciting, intimate relationship with another person, if we want to make every day fun and enjoyable, if we want jobs and careers that are passionate, we can have them.

Each person is unique and may experience passion differently, and his or her passion may arise in different realms. Freeman (1993) examined the lives of six historical figures and six living figures to determine how passion influenced their lives and motivations. He used a four-factor interactive system of human motivation consisting of biological factors—a person's preparedness; environmental factors—rewards and punishments in the system; emotional factors—mostly emotional reactions; and cognitive factors—subjective meanings individuals give situations. He found that these four variables interacted to affect passion.

Added to the initial set of sources is spirituality, which was found to be important to individuals as a basis of passion. The following are the sources of passion within individuals included in our model:

- The *Emotional Source* is our emotional response pattern. Many of us feel our passion emotionally. We find our energy when our emotions are engaged.
- The *Cognitive Source* is the subjective meaning that we place on experiences. Many of us find the realm of ideas, thinking, analysis, and synthesis a basis for passion. Our energy is high when we are using our minds.
- The *Environmental Source* is the context we are in. The environment is a catalyst for firing one's passion. Some of us need a situation conducive to a sense of enjoyment or find that we are more passionate in certain settings.
- The *Spiritual Source* is based on a drive for meaning and purpose in our lives. Some feel that we are given meaning and purpose through our spiritual source. Others feel the need to seek a higher understanding that fires our passion.

- The *Physiological Source* is related to our individual biological makeup. Each of us is innately predisposed to being more or less passionate. We all know people who are passionate all the time and across many different situations and those who are not, regardless of the situation.

Our passion arises from these sources. Passion can arise from one or more of these sources simultaneously. For example, someone has just been given an exciting, creative project that will allow him to travel to different cities and talk to interesting people in the field. In this situation, the new project may feed his emotional source in that he can be creative in his work, the ability to travel may serve as an environmental source, and being able to talk and learn from others may trigger his cognitive source. The work may be very meaningful to the person, thus engaging the spiritual source as well. For others, these conditions would not trigger their passion. Where passion arises from resides within each person and is based on what is salient to that individual.

The Five Keys to Passion

Our study identifies key factors that explain how passion develops and is sustained. These keys make up the three processes of our Passion Transformation Model.

Key #1—The Discovering Process.   Passionate people have discovered work that excites them. For some it's easy–they have known what they want to do from early in life. Others have kept journals, changed jobs, gone back to school, found a mentor, or followed career development advice to find passionate work. One person we talked to told this story.

> I was working with the poor, and committed to developing quality programs that aided clients in breaking the cycle of poverty. I was exposed to corruption, token programs and institutional politics that tied my hands so I couldn't affect policy. I left my position discouraged and disillusioned and doubted whether I could ever work in this field again. I read *What Color Is Your Parachute* [by Richard Bolles] and completed several exercises

that led me to the conclusion that I would never be happy in a job where I couldn't have impact on policy. I have returned to my line of work and I am passionate about what I do. I want my team and our clients to share similar passion and focus about their lives, too!

The first key is discovering what excites you. Looking back to times in your life when you felt passionate about something, doing self-analyses and figuring out what is really important to you, asking yourself how you would like to spend your time—all these are ways to discover your passion. Likewise, smart, forward-looking organizations find ways to help their employees discover their passion. Organizations can provide career counseling, vocational and personality testing, or opportunities for employees to develop a career path in the company.

Key #2—The Designing Process.   Passionate people find ways to make their lives exciting, meaningful, and special. Taking what they've discovered about themselves, they shape their own lives to fit it. We talked to Robert Boverie, an entrepreneur who owns his own company. Successful at a young age in the supermarket business, Robert discovered that he would be unhappy spending his life managing stores. So with a wife and four children, he quit his job and returned to school, taking enormous personal risk. It has made all the difference, because since then he has owned and operated several successful businesses. Most important, he comes to work each day passionate about what he does.

 The Designing process involves setting goals, and finding or creating environments that encourage passionate work.

Key #3—Risking.   Risk is an important part of living passionately. Those living passionately invariably have taken risks. To do otherwise is to play it safe, sit on your heels, and regret missed opportunities. For most people, the trick is to be thoughtful and intentional about risk-taking. Taking wise risks moves one toward passion and allows one to grow, but won't be devastating if unsuccessful. For some, a major risk would be to speak up in a meeting or to make a speech. For others, like Robert, a major risk would be to quit a job and go back to school. Others take risks by applying for new positions within their organizations when they occur. Organizations can be helpful in providing opportunities for individuals to take on new projects, to work in different areas, to try new skills.

People who take risks are constantly learning—about themselves and about their work. Likewise, organizations learn when their employees stretch themselves and learn new skills or concepts.

Key #4—Learning. Passionate people are always learning, reinventing themselves, and exploring new things. You must continually learn in your job to have passion. If you aren't challenged on your job, you want to either find new things to learn or move on to something new. A thirty-seven-year-old clerk told us that he is "passionate about my job when given a new challenge and allowed to be creative. I tend to lose passion when the job becomes stagnant."

People who are constantly learning are more likely to be passionate and to feel confident about their abilities. Employees who continually grow help organizations to prosper.

Key #5—Building Self-Efficacy. Self-efficacy is the belief that we have about our ability to do something. The concept of self-efficacy was developed by Albert Bandura (1982) to describe the personal beliefs we have about our ability to perform. According to Bandura, expectations of self-efficacy are the most powerful determinants of behavioral change because self-efficacy expectancies determine the initial decision to perform a behavior, the effort expended, and persistence in the face of adversity.

Self-efficacy powerfully affects our behavior. We may have the skills and talent to take on more challenging jobs, but if we believe that we are incapable of being successful, we are unlikely to apply for new positions. Positive self-efficacy is developed by trying new things and then evaluating how you did. People with low self-efficacy are unlikely to try new things, and hence lead less passionate lives. One of the most important aspects of self-efficacy is that we *can* change it from low to high. Often, taking baby steps builds self-efficacy over time.

By taking little or big steps, we are taking *risks,* as we risk we *learn,* and as we learn we develop higher *self-efficacy,* our belief in ourselves, and that we can accomplish what we set out to do. All three, working together as the *developing* process, advance our quest for a more passionate life.

Implications for Individuals and Organizations

For the Living Dead—those employees who are burned out, hate to get up in the morning, are depressed, drink too much, or find they have lost their lust for life—the Passion Transformation Model can mean a complete turnaround in their lives. It can help them discover what truly makes them happy and energized and help them to actually follow through and make changes in their lives. These changes could be within the same organization or, if they are not well suited for that employer or work, it can help them to find the work they should be doing.

All of us, at one time or another, will find our enthusiasm lagging and our work may seem like drudgery. Even if you are not burned out in your job, this model can help you learn how to keep a balance in your life between highs and lows by continually reinventing yourself and your job.

Organizations in need of a hardworking, passion-driven workforce will see the benefit of taking down barriers that are keeping people from fulfilling their passions. These organizations will develop programs, such as career development initiatives, to help their employees continually grow and learn. Organizations that are committed to employee growth will act on their promises by continually evaluating the way they do business and how it affects their employees and customers.

The outcome of the Passion Transformation Model is passionate work. By going through the three processes of Discovering, Designing, and Developing, individuals and organizations can create transformative work and workplaces. But just as important as having passion for your work is having a workplace where people love what they do, feel their work is meaningful, and have a good time doing it. A place where people support and encourage what we call Occupational Intimacy. In the next chapter we present the findings of our research regarding an "intimate" workplace and what individuals and organizations can do to foster it.

EXERCISE FOUR: Passionate Work—Your Story

In the previous chapter we asked you to think about your life as a passionate person. Now we would like you to do what we've asked hundreds of people to do through our research—to write your own story. We want you to think deeply about critical incidents—times when you were passionate about your work and times when you lost your passion for work—and to write about them. To gain the most self-knowledge through this exercise, describe what happened in detail. What were your emotions at the time and what caused them? Who were you working with and what part did they play? Describe your actual work location in detail—was it inspiring or was it deadening? Why? Write as much or as little as necessary. We have had people write pages and pages with meaning, and some who have written far less but also with powerful insight.

Once you have described your story, summarize the most important things you learned about yourself and your situation.

EXERCISE FIVE: Analyzing Your Pitfalls—Individuals

In this chapter we shared with you the four Passion Pitfalls. This exercise is designed to help you explore the pitfalls that most impact your ability to experience passionate work.

Pitfall #1—Boring or Meaningless Work.   Is your work boring? Why?

What are some creative ways to make it more interesting or different?

Is your work meaningful or meaningless? Why?

What would make your work more meaningful?

Is there hope for the future? Can your job be more interesting or meaningful? If it can, what will you do about it? If it can't, what are your alternatives?

Pitfall #2—Working in an Overly Controlled Setting.   Do you feel like you work in an overly controlled setting? Are you micromanaged by your supervisor or organizational policies and procedures?

If so, is it necessary for that much supervision or control? Some circumstances may require more oversight than others.

If it's not necessary, what are ways that you could convince your supervisor or the organization that fewer controls and less oversight are needed?

What can you do to give others confidence that they do not need to look over your shoulder or give you direction all the time?

Is there hope for the future? Can and should your job be conducted with less oversight? If it can, what will you do about it? If it can't, what are your alternatives?

Pitfall #3—Feeling Inadequate. Do you feel that you have inadequate skills, knowledge, or abilities to do the job? Do you find yourself trying to hide your mistakes? Do you feel you can't talk to anyone about your shortcomings?

If so, does that lower your enthusiasm for the job or does it increase it?

If it lowers it, what are specific things you can do to increase you feelings of adequacy? Would more training or supervision help you to do your work? Would increasingly responsible work assignments help? Would a different line of work altogether fit your personality more comfortably?

Is there hope for the future? Will you ever be able to feel adequate enough to do the job with confidence? If the potential is there, what will you do about it? What steps will you take? If the potential is just not there, what are your alternatives?

Pitfall #4—Manipulation, Dishonesty, Lack of Trust. Is manipulation, dishonesty, or lack of trust in your organization affecting the passion you have for your work? Has your supervisor/manager or coworkers ever taken credit for work you have done? Do you trust the people you work with?

If so, are you contributing to the poisonous environment or are you acting with integrity despite it? In what ways?

Are there specific things that you can do to increase the trust, integrity, and mutual support within your organization? What are they?

Is there hope for the future? Is there any potential for your work environment to become more healthy? If it can, what will you do about it? If it can't, what are your alternatives?

Other Pitfalls
Are there any other significant factors that are draining your passion for work? What are they? What can you do about them?

Ranking
Rank each of the pitfalls from 1 to 4, giving the pitfall that drains you of the most passion a "1" and the pitfall that drains the least a "4."

____Boring/Meaningless Work

____Overly Controlled Setting

____Feeling Inadequate

____Manipulation, Dishonesty, Lack of Trust

Summary
Summarize your situation. If these pitfalls are insignificant—good for you! It they are significant, however, what are the most important steps you can take to improve your situation? Can these actions make a difference? If the pitfalls are insurmountable, you should think seriously about how you can move on to another job, career, or organization.

EXERCISE SIX: Analyzing Pitfalls—Organizations

In this chapter we shared with you the four Passion Pitfalls. This exercise is designed to help you explore the pitfalls that most impact the ability of your employees to experience passionate work. Check the questions that are areas of concern for your organization.

Pitfall #1—Allowing Work to Become Boring or Meaningless.

_____Do you know of jobs that are inherently boring? Has your organization done everything possible to make them more interesting?

_____Is mundane work shared by most employees? Do some employees have more than their share?

_____Do employees complain about boring work?

_____Are employees constantly asking for new projects?

_____Do employees in some areas ask for transfers or quit their jobs more often than others?

_____Are employees doing work that means something to them? Has the organization given employees a sense of how important their work is?

Pitfall #2—Overly Controlled Settings.

_____Do your managers micromanage?

_____Is there room for mistakes to be made?

_____Are employees encouraged to take risks?

_____Does your organization have an attitude conducive to learning from mistakes and risk-taking, rather than an attitude of blaming?

_____Are employees encouraged to solve their own work problems given their own experience and knowledge?

_____Are there too many controls on employees' work?

_____Has your organization found ways to provide the right support and direction to employees given the situation? Or is it one-size-fits-all management in your organization?

Pitfall #3—Employees Feeling Inadequate.

_____Is there adequate training for employees?

_____Do employees get enough and regular feedback about their performance?

_____Is there an effective performance management system used for employee development?

_____Are employees given assignments that are appropriate to their expertise and interests?

Pitfall #4—Manipulation, Dishonesty, Lack of Trust.

_____Is there an atmosphere of mistrust in your organization?

_____Do employees ever sabotage the work?

_____Do supervisors/managers act as advocates for their employees?

_____Is credit always given where credit is due?

_____Do supervisors or managers manipulate employees?

_____Do employees manipulate each other for their own benefit?

Other Pitfalls
Are there any other significant factors that are draining your employees' passion for work? What are they? What can you do about them?

Ranking
Rank each of the Pitfalls from 1 to 4, giving the pitfall that takes the most passion out of your employees a "1" and the pitfall that takes the least a "4."

_____Boring/Meaningless Work

_____Overly Controlled Setting

_____Feeling Inadequate

_____Manipulation, Dishonesty, Lack of Trust

Summary
Summarize your situation. If these pitfalls are insignificant—good for you! It they are significant, however, what are the most important steps your organization can take to improve the situation?

Occupational Intimacy

Paul Shirley: Well in some ways maybe I've already answered that. I think when we're in a position to be able to set up such an open, whole trusting environment, we can go to extremes to be able to touch people's lives. My chart is not of a hundred and fifteen employees. In fact employees get sick of it. I show my chart of over two hundred and fifty people that are the spouses, the kids, and even grandkids that are all part of the corporate family. . . . So I think the definition begins to be—can you tear down the barriers and allow the professional tools, the competencies that you have, to intermesh with the personal competencies that each individual brings into a relationship. So now that intimacy provides a linkage and a multiplication of the capability for each of the individuals.

—PAUL SHIRLEY, cofounder of SVS

The ultimate goal of our Passion Transformation Model is the development of what we call Occupational Intimacy. Occupational Intimacy is a term we developed to represent the closeness that passionate people feel to their work. Like two passionate lovers, people in love with their work feel that it is inseparable; it is a part of who they are. They feel a sense of personal commitment to what they do. They are emotional about it, they have strong feelings of dedication, care, support, and desire associated with it. Recognition and rewards often stimulate passion for work, but many times people are so in love with their work that they would do it for the pure joy of it. Another aspect of Occupational Intimacy is the relationship one has with the people who work in the organization. Intimacy is high when the organization, the leaders, the managers, and coworkers truly care about each other and about how they do their work.

When we asked our interviewees what Occupational Intimacy meant, their answers fell into three categories: having a nurturing environment, being able to do meaningful and significant work, and having fun and loving what you do. A thirty-two-year-old training manager said Occupational Intimacy is "Developing a relationship with your job, trying to better yourself and your job situation so that you can have a long-term relationship with your job." Figure 4.1 shows the proportion of responses in each category.

Nurturing Environments

Nurture comes from the Latin word for nursing. To nurse is to provide nourishment, to care or provide for tenderly, and to cherish. To nuture is to nourish, to feed, to educate, and to rear. Passionate work environments nourish, feed, and develop employees.

FIGURE 4.1   What is Occupational Intimacy?

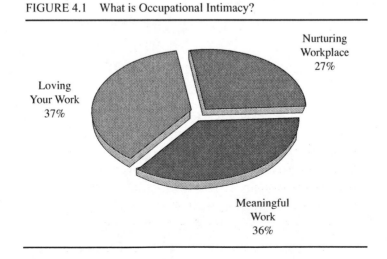

When asked what Occupational Intimacy was, 27 percent of the responses indicated it was a place where they would feel nurtured and cared for. Table 4.1a shows examples of some of these comments.

Bolman and Deal, in their book *Leading with Soul*, say the following about caring workplaces:

> Pressures of immediate tasks and the bottom line often crowd out personal needs that people bring into the workplace. Every organization is a family, whether caring or dysfunctional. Caring begins with knowing about others—it requires listening, understanding, and accepting. It progresses through a deepening sense of appreciation, respect, and ultimately, love. Love is a willingness to reach out and open one's heart. An open heart is vulnerable. Accepting vulnerability allows us to drop our masks, meet heart to heart, and be present for one another. We experience a sense of unity and delight in voluntary, human exchanges that mold the "soul of community." (1995: 103)

Organizations need to respond to this need in their employees now more than ever. Over twenty years ago, Tennov (1979) described what he called the new family—the Association. Associations are composed of unrelated people who talk to each other regularly, share their ups and downs, assemble for minor holidays and celebrations. They care for each other when in need. Our mobile society and our specialized workplaces have created these new "family" structures. The nurturing we once received primarily from our families now comes in part from our work-

TABLE 4.1a   Components of Occupational Intimacy

Nurturing Workplace
- Caring, understanding, flexible and nurturing workplace
- Caring about your work and co-workers
- Have respect for employees ideas
- Get to know employees as people
- Listen to employees' ideas and respect them
- Understand and have compassion for our humanness
- Really care about the people

---

places. Robert, the entrepreneur we mentioned in Chapter 3 who owns an international business with his wife, said:

> We *are* the company and so, unlike what I always thought was a good thing to do in my previous business life, we do have a personal relationship with our employees. . . . We get involved in some of their personal issues that frankly are none of our business, you know, but we don't think about it that way now.

The Dalai Lama talks about the importance of finding nurturing and meaningful relationships *everywhere*.

> Basing our relationship on the qualities of affection, compassion, and mutual respect as human beings. Basing a relationship on these qualities enables us to achieve a deep and meaningful bond not only with our lover or spouse but also with friends, acquaintances, or strangers—virtually any human being. It opens up unlimited possibilities and opportunities for connection." (HH Dalai Lama and Cutler 1998: 112)

One of our interviewees, a filmmaker, talked about the differences between the arts and organizations.

> The film business, like theater, it's a very family kind of thing where you come together and you care for each other more deeply than if you were all working together at Blockbuster or something like that. It really is more of a sharing than I found in other work. And I mean people just genuinely care for each other and there's an amount of collaboration that happens in the film business and in the theater where you have to have some amount of openness. You have to be able to listen and you have to be able to give when it's time, where there's time, for there to be new ideas, things like that. And I think in most businesses there aren't those things. There's a hierarchy and you do your job and when your job is done, you go away. [If] you don't get your job done, screw it. You come back the next day and you get back into it. Where film and theater just aren't that way. There's an emergency and an immediacy to the arts that doesn't exist in the rest of the workday world.

A community college educator we talked to said, "Occupational Intimacy is a positive, nurturing environment in which employees can grow and achieve their personal goals as well as provide good services for the organization and be recognized for doing so." Another interviewee said that Occupational Intimacy is "Caring, understanding and flexibility in the workplace."

Meaningful Work

When asked what Occupational Intimacy was, 36 percent of the responses indicated it was a place where they were doing work that was meaningful to themselves, the organization, and society. Table 4.1b shows examples of some of these comments. One of our interviewees

TABLE 4.1b   Components of Occupational Intimacy

Meaningful Work
- Have successful, high quality programs that produce results and make our work meaningful
- Build measurable components where employees can see results
- Knowing you are an essential part of the work
- Being able to make a difference
- Sharing in success and feedback
- Knowing exactly what you do and how your work affects others
- Work contribution is special

said, "I have a hard time getting involved in activities when I cannot see their purpose or usefulness."

Bolman and Deal, talking about the importance of having meaningful work, said, "When people feel a sense of efficacy and an ability to influence their world, they seek to be productive. They direct their energy and intelligence toward making a contribution rather than obstructing progress" (1995: 107).

In his book *The Passionate Organization*, Lucas describes the key elements of passionate workplaces:

- *People have to feel the goal matters.* There has to be awareness that the results of our efforts will have a significant impact. Will life be better if we do this well?
- *There has to be true ownership.* This mission can't be partly ours and partly someone else's. Everything else aside, is this ours to win or lose?
- *People have to believe that the goal could not be achieved without them.* Their labors, their sacrifices, their united effort is needed. Ultimately, heroic efforts are about responsibility, accountability, and duty. What will happen if we fail?
- *There has to be some sense of urgency.* Something important has to rest on the timing of the outcome. The clock is about to run out. Our competitors are about to go to market with a similar product. Do we have what it takes to win?
- *People have to understand that "great goal" doesn't automatically translate to "bigger goal."* Stretch goals are not necessarily numerical goals. Will this effort change things, even if we can't quantify it now or later? (1999: 102)

Robert, the entrepreneur we mentioned earlier, said "I believe that passion has to do with actually liking what you do and having a vision about what you do, so that you work for some sort of purpose rather than just plodding along day by day."

Loving Your Work

When asked what Occupational Intimacy was, 37 percent of the responses indicated it was doing work they loved and having fun. A twenty-five-year-old retail manager said, "Occupational intimacy is actually loving your job. Looking forward to going to work and knowing exactly what you do and how you effect others through what you do." Table 4.1c shows examples of some of these comments.

When we are doing work we love, we are excited, motivated, happy, and have a sense of pride and accomplishment. People have worked under dire and daunting circumstances just to be able to do the work they love. We can use Southwest Airlines again as an example.

When the people of Southwest dress in a fun style, their work becomes play. When you're having fun at work it doesn't feel like work at all; it's better than tolerable, it's enjoyable. Having a job that's fun is certainly worth holding onto; people are more likely to accept ownership of their responsibilities, and much more inclined to go the extra mile and do whatever it takes. Stories of going above and beyond or doing whatever it takes are a dime a dozen at Southwest. (Freiberg and Freiberg 1996: 205)

TABLE 4.1c   Components of Occupational Intimacy

Loving Your Work
- I absolutely live for customer satisfaction
- Constant challenge and learning experience
- Knowing how to do your job and loving it
- I love imparting knowledge to others
- Excited at the thought of what I could do
- I love seeing the light go on

When we are doing work we love, time seems to fly and we are totally involved in what we are doing. Mihaly Csikszentmihalyi (1990) describes this as "flow." Flow is experienced when we are doing work we know we can accomplish, for which we have the time and space to complete, that we know exactly what we are doing, and we receive immediate feedback. We are so engrossed in this work that our troubles and preoccupation with ourselves disappear. We feel in control of our work. When we are in flow, time seems to become altered and we lose track of it. People who love their work find themselves in a state of flow more often than those who are watching the clock, waiting for the day to end.

Nurturing, meaningfulness, and fun create a sense of intimacy with our work. One person we interviewed described Occupational Intimacy:

The more you learn about a topic, how much more exciting the topic is, the more you get connected to it or if you'd like, intimate with it. It just snowballs, it just fascinates, at least it does for me in amazing ways. . . . I think as trust builds and to me it's about people coming together and feeling like they connect, . . . that you have the sense that your participation is making a difference. There's having an impact on how people think and what actually happens in the organization. What a wonderful idea. I'd like to think that people can participate and that there is evidence that they are affecting other people and affecting the practices and the policies that go on there. So I would think that all of that would enhance this sense of intimacy as well. I mean, the more you get to know another person . . . the more interesting that person becomes, and the more you want to spend time with that person, find out more and get even more connected. So, it just feels right to me.

Another one of our interviewees said, "I think to the extent that we foster a sense of wide-awareness and mindfulness, we can rejuvenate people about their work and about their sense of intimacy and the work place. . . . In very powerful ways, [we] can make a difference in how connected you feel and how excited you are about that work."

Intimacy

Intimate relationships involve interdependence—usually frequent, strong, emotional, and lasting connections based on mutual and interlocking needs. Intimacy requires vulnerability. Often it cannot proceed and grow without self-disclosure. Being intimate means sharing personal information—hopes, dreams, fears, doubts, and risky "secrets" that could impact one's life, career, or relationship—which would not otherwise be shared unless with a trusted confidant. "Intimacy means that we can be who we are in a relationship, and allow the other person to do the same," according to Harriet Goldhor Lerner in *The Dance of Intimacy* (3). That requires that we can talk honestly about what is important to us, to express emotion, and to share deep personal truths with another person.

Intimacy grows over time, as relationships are tested and proven sound and emotional attachment increases. Intimacy decreases when trust is betrayed, when intimate information is no longer willingly shared, or when the emotional bond is weakened. Living with another person does not ensure intimacy. Stories abound about spouses in long-term relationships who "go through the motions" but find intimacy outside the marriage. Intimate relationships are varied. They can occur between best friends, sexual partners, family members, or

TABLE 4.1d   Components of Occupational Intimacy

Nurturing Workplace	Meaningful Work	Loving Your Work
• Caring, understanding, flexible and nurturing workplace	• Have successful, high quality programs that produce results and make our work meaningful	• I absolutely live for customer satisfaction
• Caring about your work and co-workers	• Build measurable components where employees can see results	• Constant challenge and learning experience
• Have respect for employees' ideas	• Knowing you are an essential part of the work	• Knowing how to do your job and loving it
• Get to know employees as people	• Being able to make a difference	
• Listen to employees' ideas and respect them	• Sharing in success and feedback	• I love imparting knowledge to others
• Understand and have compassion for our humanness	• Knowing exactly what you do and how your work affects others	• Excited at the thought of what I could do
• Really care about the people	• Work contribution is special	• I love seeing the light go on

coworkers. Sometimes intimacy is quickly established, often through circumstance—a tragedy for instance, but intimacy often requires time to grow.

"Playing hard to get" can increase desire for another person; likewise, the lack of barriers can lessen passion. Intimacy is also dependent on continuous growth, learning, and change. "The worst enemy of the intimacy component of love is stagnation. Although people want some predictability from a loving relationship, too much predictability will probably undermine the intimacy experienced in a close relationship. Hence, it is necessary to introduce some elements of change and variation to keep the relationship alive and growing" (Sternberg 1987: 95). Always keeping an even keel in a relationship maintains calm but could also cause the relationship to suffer because it lacks excitement or adventure.

Relationships fill basic needs that people have. Those needs include the need for intimacy—closeness, the need for social integration—sharing with others, the need to nurture—taking care of others, the need for assistance—receiving help from others, and the need for reassurance of our own worth (Weiss 1969). People have the same needs at work and these can be met to some degree in the workplace. When we ask employees to give us their all but to leave their vulnerabilities or needs at home, we are not respecting the whole person. In fact, how can employees give their all if part of them has been left behind, if the part that's willing to be open despite the chance of getting hurt is not allowed to surface?

Occupational Intimacy

What we know about intimacy and relationships helps us to understand this concept of Occupational Intimacy. We again draw on Sternberg's (1987) work on love and relationships. Sternberg used the concept of a triangle to illustrate the components of relationships. For Sternberg, an equilateral triangle with the components of passion, intimacy, and commitment was the prototype of the ideal relationship (see Figure 4.2).

Depending, then, on how much passion, intimacy, and commitment exists in a relationship, various triangles can be constructed to illustrate these types. A relationship heavy with infatuation or heavy emotional involvement illustrates a passionate relationship. A relationship based

FIGURE 4.2 Sternberg's Triangle of Love

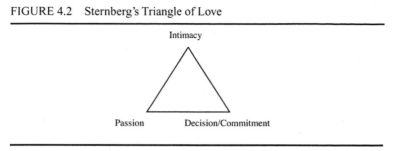

SOURCE: Sternberg 1988: 37.

on intimacy to a great extent would have friendship and caring as its main component. A relationship based primarily on commitment would stress sticking together until the goal is achieved (see Figure 4.3).

FIGURE 4.3 Sternberg's Shape of Triangles as a Function of Kind of Love

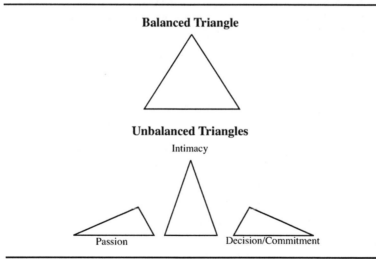

SOURCE: Sternberg 1988: 72.

We can use the same triangular illustrations to describe the various types of Occupational Intimacy in the workplace. True Occupational Intimacy would look like the equilateral triangle of the ideal relationship, with meaningful work, nurturing environment, and love of work now as the elements. Meaningful Work (MW) and Love of Work (LW) are the components of Passionate Work. Occupational Intimacy is formed by

FIGURE 4.4   Occupational Intimacy Triangle

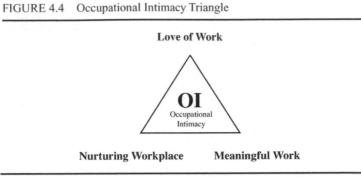

adding a Nurturing Workplace (NW) to Passionate Work (MW + LW) (see Figure 4.4). Intimacy is a two-way street, a give and take between two parties. Someone could love what they do and find it meaningful but would not feel intimate or close to their workplace if the organization did not care about them or their work.

Overlaying the organization's actual emphasis on the ideal triangle would illustrate the degree to which Occupational Intimacy is present and what it is most characterized by—nurturing, meaningfulness, or love of work. The closer to the ideal, the higher the OI.

A very nurturing and caring organization would be skewed as in Figure 4.5. In this type of organization employees would have great team spirit or feel like they were family. The work itself would be secondary to relationships. Individuals might enjoy the closeness but find the work tedious and routine. An example is a fast-food restaurant where management really cares about the employees but employees see their job only as a stepping-stone. The work is not meaningful enough to keep their passion for it alive (see Figure 4.5).

FIGURE 4.5   Nurturing Workplace

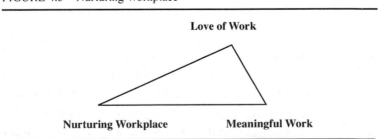

FIGURE 4.6   Meaningful Work

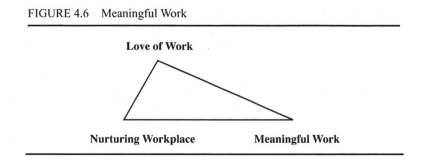

In Figure 4.6, the work has importance to the employee or society but soon comes to be viewed as a duty or obligation. Without mutual caring and a sense of enjoyment, employees find that the job weighs them down. This happens often in nonprofit or public sector organizations. We have talked to many teachers who felt their work was important but they were unsatisfied with how they were treated by administration, parents, and students. One thirteen-year veteran of teaching told us

> There are so many barriers—schools that are too large, lack of funding for adequate materials, lack of opportunities for professional development that are fully paid and time off for the event is given without having to take a personal or sick leave day, lack of substantial time for collaboration with other professionals, lower salaries, lack of parental involvement, poor image of education and educators that is perpetuated in the media, a superintendent that has not yet visited some of the schools in his district. All of these lead to low morale for those who choose to remain in teaching.

A sense of duty kept these teachers dedicated to their jobs but they were very unhappy overall.

The last triangle, Figure 4.7, illustrates an environment where fun and a sense of enjoyment is stressed. Employees have a great time at work but it loses its luster after a while if the work is routine and they feel uncared for by management. The teachers we mentioned above loved their work—the actual teaching, but lost passion because they were not cared for. After both owning a restaurant and working in the nightclub busi-

FIGURE 4.7   Love of Work

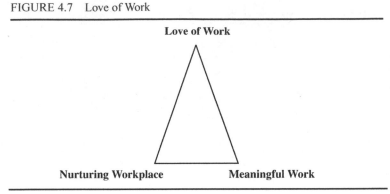

ness, we saw another aspect of a fun workplace. In these environments, employees had a great time and made easy money, but the work seemed meaningless and most waitpeople or bartenders felt they could be replaced without any trouble. In recreational businesses the employees often find they come to work to pal around with their coworkers and enjoy what they do tremendously, but feel like they aren't making a contribution to society, or that the organization really cares about them.

An organization that was nurturing (NW) and fun (LW) but has little meaning could be called an *Indulgent* Environment. Usually these would be low-level jobs that are merely stepping-stones to better occupations. An organization high in fun (LW) and meaningful work (MW) but with little nurturing could be called a *Compelling* Environment. Here employees love what they do and want to continue but feel the organization doesn't care about them. Artists, scientists, or college professors might fall into this group. An environment where nurturing (NW) and meaningful work (MW) were high but were low on fun could be labeled an *Affirming* Environment. Examples where one might find this environment are schools, small departments within larger organizations, or secretarial/administrative work (see Figure 4.8).

How do we create organizations that have all three components—nurturing, fun, and meaningfulness—which make up Occupational Intimacy? To do this, it is necessary to work toward filling the needs of both individuals and organizations.

FIGURE 4.8   Occupational Intimacy Environments

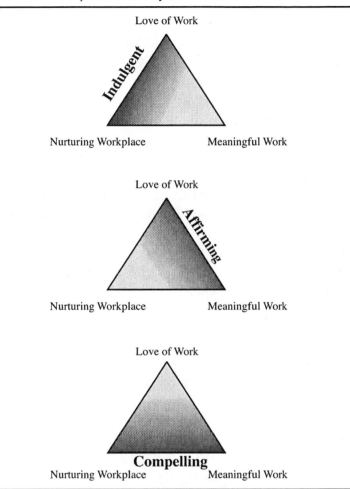

Human and Organizational Needs

Since people are the building blocks of organizations, the success of an organization depends on the relationship between the needs of the people and the needs of the organization. Organizations need people for their talent, their energy, and their effort; people need organizations for the rewards they provide. These rewards are intrinsic (for example, important work, creative outlets), extrinsic (such as salary, benefits), or social (affiliation, social integration). Researchers have shown that the needs of the organization and the needs of the individuals in that organization are not always well aligned (Argyris 1964). "When the fit between people and organizations is poor, one or both suffers: individuals may feel neglected or oppressed, and organizations sputter because individuals withdraw their efforts or even work against organizational purposes" (Bolman and Deal 1997: 119).

Passion is related to our needs: our needs to grow, to learn, and to be involved in pursuits that feed our passion. Passion feeds passion. Passion is experienced both in the head and the heart, known as well as felt. Passion can be nurtured or starved. "The connection to personal passion and destiny must be a physical one, felt in the gut. This kind of living relationship with personal passion can be extremely difficult in the antiseptic environment of a modern office. Its clean lines do not easily reflect the hidden pulses of human longing and remembrance" (Whyte 1994: 158).

Results of Occupational Intimacy

Why should we strive for Occupational Intimacy? Is it worth the effort? Although organizations have survived without it in the past, the days when organizations can ignore the human aspects of their employees are over. The workplace is changing rapidly. Women and minorities now comprise over half of the workforce and their presence has changed occupational roles and policies dramatically, (such as flex hours, flex time, distributed work, and so forth). This has led toward the recognition and importance of the emotional and spiritual aspects of individuals—our soft side. On a larger scale, cultural change is happening worldwide. The way we use language and how we portray ourselves needs to change as well. For years women have existed within the brotherhood of all mankind. Now it is being described as "The Sisterhood of Man" (Peterson 1996: 275). With the mix of so many cultures in the workplace the status quo is not sustainable over time.

In his book *The Future of Work,* Grantham talks about the new workplace. He calls it *work as community* (2000: 32). He points out that "communities as networks of people around us are the fundamental social and psychological link between our work activities and the rest of our lives" (33). As individuals, we seek intimacy as a basic need and drive. Intimacy provides us with feelings of being cared for, needed, loved, and connected with others. If this is what people seek, organizations must also help the individuals they are comprised of to fulfill their needs. Just as individuals seek intimacy and emotional connectedness with others, so in organizations employees seek connections with their fellow employees and to their work. They want to feel needed and cared for, just as they do in their private lives. If this happens, employees are apt to have more loyalty, greater motivation, and a true commitment to what the organization is trying to accomplish. Ultimately, greater production will occur if employees love what they do, do it in a place that cares about them, and when they feel they are making a difference.

Highly successful companies have proven that when there is a good fit between organizational and individual needs, both parties prosper and grow (Waterman 1994). Waterman's book, *What America Does Right* (1994), is focused on the relationship between organizations and people. Successful companies tend to view the organization as a family made up of individuals who have needs, feelings, biases, talents, and personalities. He contends that we need to pay attention to the needs of the individuals in the organization as well as to the needs of the organization. This reinforces an organizational imperative to foster diversity in the workplace and to then tap into the multiplicity of passions that reside in workers of all persuasions and experiences.

Serious problems can occur when an organization does not respond to these various needs. In Figure 4.9 we illustrate just three of the paths available. Two of these paths pose real problems for organizations. These illustrate the patterns we discussed in Chapter 3 of Passion Extinction, Passion Hopping, and Passion Renewal.

Passion Hopping

From the research on the new workforce (Bova and Kroth 2001; Grantham 2000) we know that Gen Xers as a group are interested in continual learning, fast promotions, close work relationships, and an enjoyable work environment. Owing to the demographics of the work-

FIGURE 4.9   Once Developed, Passion May Follow One of Three Paths

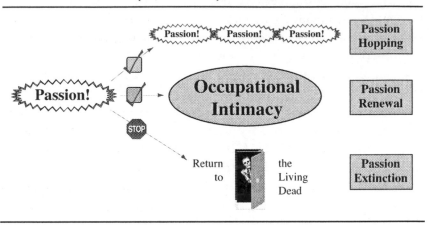

place, these employees can expect to be fully employed—free agents in the workplace. Loyalty is not a major concern for these individuals. We can expect them to move from job to job if they do not find what they want in one particular organization. They will stay passionate simply because of the continuous learning and rate of change.

Other generations can also display Passion Hopping behavior. The Nexters who are soon to enter the workforce are predicted to have similar behaviors and values of Gen X. Older employees will find they can now enter new and different work environments easily because of the shortage of qualified employees.

Passion Extinction

The bulk of the workplace today is made up of Baby Boomers, with an average age of forty-four.

These employees are extremely varied in how they have approached work and life. Some of them came out of the sixties and seventies as free thinkers—very creative and productive. Others are driven by success and wealth—labeled Yuppies. And some of these employees are working in positions they just drifted into, rather than jobs they chose. They see retirement as something their parents have but they may never have. The road before them may seem long and uneventful. These people–often

Baby Boomers, but also coming from any generation–are the living dead of organizations. We all know them and hope not to become one of them.

Passion Renewal

There are others who love what they do, find fulfillment in their work, and find themselves doing their work in an environment that cares about them. They have found passionate work and Occupational Intimacy. Renewers cross all groups and have in common the ability to know themselves, know what work they want to do, and know how to maintain and sustain their passion. Lucas outlines what organizations will have to do to keep valuable employees who stay from becoming the living dead.

> The organization that wins in the twenty-first century will focus its attention on passion. It will find, develop, and articulate a vision for which all of its people will be willing to fight long and hard. It will only hire people who are passionate by nature, and especially passionate about its vision. It will methodically and quickly cut out the deadwood—including the really smart people who don't believe. At the same time, it will prize originality and feistiness and diversity and even the offbeat, and it will loathe the status quo and "one best way" and things that look like everything else. It will emphasize inspiring vision, big purpose, deeply-held core values, mutual trust, and stretch goals more than planning and learning. (1999: 66)

Occupational Intimacy can result from transforming work. With a changing population, an aging workforce, and futures that cannot be predicted, creating environments to foster loyalty and commitment in employees will become more important than ever.

Barriers to Occupational Intimacy

If a workplace where Occupational Intimacy exists creates happy, motivated employees, why doesn't it exist everywhere? We can look to the backbone of the American workplace and the forces that shaped our society.

History

For centuries, the Puritan work ethic has been the unspoken rule of thumb for how organizations should treat their employees. In this view, employees are expected to give a full day's work for a full day's pay. They are not expected to have fun, relax, or really even enjoy what they do. If they do as they are told they might go far. Emotions are things that should be dealt with at home and not at the workplace. That includes both positive and negative emotions. And they should never, never let a personal problem interfere with their work.

The Scientific Management theory by Frederick Winslow Taylor at the turn of the century also influenced how organizations valued employees. Taylor's theory helped push the growth of industry in the United States by developing efficient processes and procedures. But the welfare of employees was a secondary concern. Employees were seen as a resource that could easily be replaced. Scientific Management theory sought to organize and plan every detail of work to maximize efficiency and effectiveness. The time and motion studies and "improvements" of this movement sucked the humanity out of the workplace.

The Puritan work ethic combined with Scientific Management benefited organizations to the detriment of the individual worker. These were decades where workers, almost entirely men, poured their life into their work and hardly knew their own children or wives. There was no intersection between home and work, and work came before home.

There are approximately 77 million baby boomers now in the workplace, many of whom watched their fathers work long hours, come home to dinner, read the paper, and watch TV, leaving hardly any time for the family. Because these boomers missed out on that intimacy, they are seeking it now. They are fighting against the system that came out of the strict work ethic and management practices that devalued individuals. And they are a powerful voice.

Relationships

For decades, our society devalued the importance of close relationships, especially in the workplace. Although we spend most of our waking hours at work, these relationships at work have been discouraged. Nevertheless, people everywhere are seeking connection and better relationships with others. Our media reminds us in every song, news story, and even television commercial how people are trying to find friends, lovers, and partners.

Our mobile society makes it difficult to maintain close relationships. Relationships take time and effort and if it isn't easy, humans tend to take the route of least resistance—the easy way out. We have become a nation of specialists—doing specific jobs in specific places, without the input of many other individuals. We can now do our work from our homes through technology. There are many naysayers out there who predict the doom of relationships because of technology. Children now spend many of their waking hours in front of a computer screen instead of playing team sports or tag in the front yard or spending time with friends. Adults come home from work and instead of relating to family, sit at the computer reading e-mail, shopping, or playing games by themselves. At work we are guilty of trying to have most of our meetings by e-mail instead of face-to-face, even though our colleagues are just down the hall.

Leadership

Leadership, however, is probably the most important factor contributing to the presence or absence of Occupational Intimacy. The leaders of organizations set the vision, mission, values, and the culture of the organization. When leadership does not value the importance of human needs, then humanistic values are absent from the organization. Figure 4.10 shows the influence employees have on the level of passion in an organization. Top management, through its ability to set the vision, design the structure, and create the overall culture, has the greatest impact. Middle management has a role through its ability to give rewards and recognition, design jobs, and help employees develop. Employees have much less effect on the overall passion level but do impact it through their own personal level of passion. Leaders have so much influence that without their support even grass-root efforts to make the workplace more humane usually fail.

There are leaders such as Paul Shirley, cofounder of SVS, who strive to make the workplace more connected to the whole person. "Why is it that

FIGURE 4.10   Ability to Influence Passion in the Organization

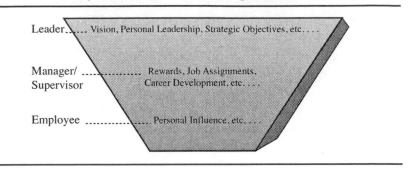

you can't have an environment where your spiritual life, your family life and your professional life intercept to the maximum level possible?" he asks. In building his company, Shirley tried to incorporate these various aspects of life into the organization. He says, "Okay, let's take a close look at what's important to me spiritually, and what I'm about from a faith perspective, and then, as I enter into relationships with people in the work environment there is always an aspect of that." Developing leaders who are passionate and who inspire passion in others is imperative for organizations that wish to succeed.

Occupational Intimacy is what organizations should strive to promote to best serve their self-interest. The organizations that succeed will be places where people are doing work they love and where there is two-way caring between employees and the organization. Leider and Shapiro described this situation when they wrote, "In the perfect job, you're applying the talents you enjoy most to an interest you're passionate about, in an environment that fits who you are and what you value" (1995: 94).

This chapter opened with a quote from Paul Shirley about his view of Occupational Intimacy. Shirley was one of the three cofounders of SVS, an aeronautics technology organization that went from initial startup capital of $3,000 in 1993 to one of the fastest growing technology companies in the country by 1999. In our interview with Paul he talked about the type of company he and his partners set out to create.

We'd like to be involved in something that was fun, first and foremost. And second, we'd like to be involved in something that makes a difference, in some form. And that's a real vague term, making a difference, but it was something that we all certainly felt was important, whether it was making a difference in people's lives or making a difference in technology or making a difference in National Defense, but make a difference. And I was so excited, I truly went home that night to tell my wife about [this, saying] "this is so cool, . . . we're going to rock and roll, we're going to have some fun, make a difference." And she said, "How are we going to pay the bills?" That's when we added to our vision, "oh by the way, make a profit." To ride a high technology environment where everyone can have fun, make a difference, and oh by the way, make a profit.

This emphasis on the relationship between employees and organizations is at the crux of Organizational Intimacy. To be successful we need to examine the needs and limitations of both individuals and organizations and to strive to develop processes, programs, values, and policies that reinforce the relationship rather than deny it. In Chapters 5, 6, and 7 we will look at ways organizations and individuals can move toward Occupational Intimacy.

EXERCISE SEVEN: Occupational Intimacy—Individual

Occupational Intimacy is the closeness that people feel to their work. People who are passionate about their work—they enjoy what they do and it is meaningful—and who are also cared for and nurtured by their organization, experience Occupational Intimacy. This exercise asks you to consider how intimate you are with your work.

Love of Work

Do you enjoy your work? Is the work itself fun? What would make your work more fun?

What would have to change to add fun to the workplace?

> What would the organization have to do?
> What would you have to do?

Meaningfulness of Work

Are you doing important work?

What would have to change to make your work more meaningful?

What would the organization have to do?

What would you have to do?

Nurturing Organization

Does your organization care for you, support you, develop you, make you feel important?

What would have to change to help you feel nurtured by your employer?

> What would the organization have to do?
> What would you have to do?

Overall, what is your current level of Occupational Intimacy?

____High

____Medium

____Low

EXERCISE EIGHT: Occupational Intimacy—Organizations

Occupational Intimacy is the closeness that people feel to their work. People who are passionate about their work—they enjoy what they do and it is meaningful—and who are also cared for and nurtured by their organization, experience Occupational Intimacy. This exercise asks you to look at how well your organization supports Occupational Intimacy.

Rate your current organization high (H), medium (M), or low (L) for each question.

Work That Is Joyful and Fun (H, M, or L)

____Does your organization try to create a healthy, cheerful atmosphere?

____Are employees allowed to have fun as they work?

____Is the workplace a visually stimulating environment?

____Does management try to lighten things up routinely?

What is your organization doing well in providing an enjoyable environment?

What are the current barriers to doing this well?

What are some steps your organization could take to create a more enjoyable environment?

Work That Is Meaningful (H, M, or L)

____Does your organization try to create meaningful work?

____Do employees know how their work contributes to the overall goals of the organization?

____Does the organization have a compelling mission and vision?

____Are employees encouraged to add their own creativity to their work?

____Has the organization found ways to link employees' personal goals with organizational goals?

What is your organization doing well in this area?

What are the current barriers to doing this?

What are some steps your organization could take to create more meaningful work for your employees?

Nurturing Work Environment (H, M, or L)

____Does your organization "nurture" your employees?

____Do employees feel cared about by the organization?

____Is there a team spirit in your organization?

____Are employees seen as individuals (instead of as objects) by the organization?

____Are individual circumstances taken into account when dealing with employees?

____Does the organization let employees know how important they are to the success of the organization?

What is your organization doing well in this area?

What are the current barriers to doing these things?

What are some steps your organization could take to create more meaningful work for your employees?

Overall
Overall, how would you rate how well your organization supports Occupational Intimacy?

____High

____Medium

____Low

Summary
List two to five of the most important things your organization could work on that would dramatically improve Occupational Intimacy for your employees:

The Discovering Process

Knowing other people is intelligence, knowing yourself is wisdom. Overcoming others takes strength, overcoming yourself takes greatness.

—Lao Tzu, The Tao Te Ching

Discovering Process
Organization Individual

**Discovering
Enabling Processes**

Goal
Develop understanding
of factors affecting
level of passion

When I went into teaching, it was purely by default. Although I came to love K-12 work—I loved it more for the doors it opened for me. Discovering I could be an effective administrator came next. But then I truly came to life when I discovered I could invent processes to enable adults to learn and, can also roll them out. I learned that I enjoy thinking systematically and designing whole organizational change. . . . My 18-year-old-self is grateful for my more confident 40-year-old self.

—Eileen Allison, educational consultant

Discovering

The first process is *Discovering*. Many of the world's most powerful, enduring stories involve the discovery of passionate work. In the Christian world, Paul's trip to Damascus is an example of profound discovery. On that trip Paul found his purpose in life after scales that blinded him fell from his eyes. Joan of Arc is said to have heard a voice from as early as childhood that revealed her purpose in life. The Buddha "went into solitude and then sat beneath the bo tree, the tree of immortal knowledge, where he received an illumination that has enlightened all of Asia for twenty-five hundred years" (Campbell 1988: 167). This chapter will discuss the goal of discovering, the elements of discovering, the reasons we don't discover, what we are trying to discover, and transformation theory.

Discovering can be an *evolutionary* process as one learns more and more about the world and about him- or herself; or it can be a *revolutionary,* sudden, powerful, mind-and-heart-changing experience. Discovering can be *intentional*—occurring via purposeful contemplation, reflection, or experiential testing; or it can happen to us, be *imposed* when events such as divorce, death of a loved one, a new baby, a health problem, or being fired from a job cause us to think about life differently.

Imposed discovery, which forces a person to question assumptions about life ("I thought I'd work here for thirty years." "I didn't realize this technology would be obsolete so soon." "I really believed that my marriage would last a lifetime."), is often traumatic, difficult to adjust to, and unexpected. One woman gave us an example of imposed discovery when she said "My boyfriend and I became too serious and I accidentally became pregnant. I quickly realized that I had to grow up—I became an adult that day. I suddenly became passionate about the responsibility of caring for a child and the desire to be a good mother."

Intentional discovery is often exciting, informational, incremental, and can be a way of life. Discovery that just seems to happen to us—because it's imposed through life situations or serendipitously like Paul's epiphany—can be highly emotional, sudden, and intensely life changing. Both are opportunities for learning and growth.

Discovering should be a joyous process. Hamel and Prahalad say:

There beats in every person the heart of an explorer. The joy of discovery may be found in the pages of a new cookbook, in a brochure of exotic vacations, in an architect's plans for a custom-built home, in the trek to a remote trout stream, in the first run down a virgin-powdered ski slope, or in the birth of a child. (1994: 145)

Are you irresistibly drawn to your vocation? Does your work delight you? Do you revel in your work? Are you excited about learning more about yourself and what you really want to do, or does it frighten you?

Discovering has always been a deeply emotional process. It involves fear, treading on unknown, possibly dangerous territory; excitement, adventuring into new relationships, new fields of knowledge, learning new ways of doing things; loss, being uprooted from familiar surroundings; and hope, anticipating possibilities for the future. In *The Discoverers*, Daniel J. Boorstin says, "The most promising works ever written on the maps of human knowledge are *terra incognita*—unknown territory" (1985: xvi). Throughout the ages, the first step to discovering new lands was often simply acknowledging that there was a world waiting to be discovered, that knowledge was not finite, that everything under the sun hadn't been invented, and that there were differing spiritual practices, peoples, or personal experiences waiting to be found.

In fact, throughout history, the most significant constraint to discovery may have been prior knowledge. Though this seems counterintuitive, current knowledge blinds people, and indeed has blinded entire societies to uncharted territories of land, relationship, and self-knowledge. Boorstin says, "The greatest obstacle to discovering the shape of the earth, the continents, and the ocean was not ignorance but the illusion of knowledge" (1983: 86) or, in other words, the belief that current knowledge was "the truth." Subsequent discoveries, often at great personal or societal price, proved those "truths" to be mere belief-system placeholders. "Only against the forgotten backdrop of the received common sense and myths of their time," says Boorstin, "can we begin to sense the courage, the rashness, the heroic and imaginative thrusts of the great discoverers. They had to battle against the current 'facts' and dogmas of the learned" (xv).

Recognizing that something is amiss or doesn't make sense or that what we thought was writ in concrete, isn't, is often the first step to discovery. Thomas Kuhn, writing about scientific evolution and revolution, said, "Discovery commences with the awareness of anomaly, i.e., with the recognition that nature has somehow violated the paradigm-induced expectations that govern normal science. It then continues with a more or less extended exploration of the area of the anomaly. And it closes only when the paradigm theory has been adjusted so that the anomalous has become the expected" (1962: 52–53). Kuhn describes the resistance of scientific communities over the years to new theoretical concepts. If it is difficult for scientists, who are supposed to be professional discoverers, to revise their own worldviews, how difficult must it be for the rest of us?

Another way to look at how limiting these cognitive blinders can be is to think about how people close their minds off to possibilities. Young people limit their aspirations, often unconsciously, because of the signals that society, peers, or parents may send them. Corporations become defunct because they stick to a formula for success and ignore new ways of thinking. Successful companies are always searching for new possibilities, building on old successes yet able to discard ways of doing things that are out of date. As Zen Master Suzuki says, "In the beginner's mind there are many possibilities, but in the experts there are few" (1970: 21). How many of us have retained that open, inquisitive, pensive, eager, beginner's mind? How many of us, having found habits of success or survival, are living on autopilot rather than searching for what makes work passionate?

Goal of the Discovering Process for Individuals

Discovering is the process in which an individual comes to know what she or he is passionate about doing. This process is iterative and should continue throughout a lifetime. Even if a person has "seen the light" and seems to know what really excites her about work, continual inner work intended to maintain awareness is critical to sustain that passion. Ongoing critical reflection and study must continue in order to understand the sources of one's passion, to recognize when it is waning, and to explore either the incremental or quantum changes required to sustain or increase it. This vigilance is required lest over a lifetime the perceived passion slowly, often unconsciously, devolves into just surviving.

If you are unhappy with your work, you can either change the work itself—get a new job, rearrange the work you are already doing; or you can change you—your attitude, how you view the work, and what you want to accomplish with the work you are doing. Either can be effective. Either might be the more appropriate in a given situation. The trick is to take charge—to not let the unhappy situation dominate, but to proactively discover what it is that will make you most passionate in any given circumstance.

The ultimate goal of Discovering for individuals is to find your own intense passion, to find the music that already resides inside you and that is waiting to be heard from you.

Goal of the Discovering Process for Organizations

The ultimate goal of Discovering for organizations is to have employees who know what they love to do and who are doing it. Discovering for organizations means providing ways for employees to determine the kind of work that produces their best efforts, their most creativity, and the highest quality of work. If your organization is unhappy with the motivation of the workforce, you can continue to depend on the tried and true that got you this far—perhaps a command-and-control structure, tight oversight, and traditional job progression. Or you can change your approach—your attitude about employees, how you view their work, how you will motivate them, and what opportunities to learn you will give them. To be effective, an organization must first have a clear idea of its own mission, vision, and culture—in other words to discover its own passion; and second to find, hire, motivate, develop, and retain key talent by helping *them* attain and sustain passion for the organization and its work over time.

Who Is Responsible for Discovering in Organizations?

The person most responsible for the Discovering process in organizations is the executive leader. Inspirational leaders are the keepers of organizational mission and vision. Senior leaders capture the visions of people within and outside the organization, using them to enrich their own views, and then execute decisions designed to fulfill their desired future for the organization. According to Hamel and Prahalad, "Senior management teams compete in the acquisition of industry foresight" (1994: 83). Dedicating significant time to create a view of the future, they claim, is essential to remaining competitive over time. Once the desired future becomes tangible, executives have the task of building organizational capability to achieve their strategic intent. To create that future, ". . . An entire company, not just a few isolated boffins or 'research fellows,' must possess industry foresight" (87). Industry foresight, they say, requires a deep and boundless curiosity and a childlike innocence about what could and should be.

Having discovered an inspiring purpose and proposed organizational future, leaders can then connect them to intrinsic and extrinsic motivators for individuals throughout the organization.

Middle and first line management also play a key role in the process of discovery in organizations. These leaders are the primary facilitators of Discovering for their employees. Supervisors can be serious about employee developmental and career planning or they can give it lip service. Poor supervisors may be the top reason talented employees leave an organization. Good supervisors create personal loyalty at a time when loyalty to the organization has become passé.

Human resource development practitioners are a third source of Discovering in an organization. HRD professionals provide systems for Discovering that include career development planning, leadership development, and succession planning. HRD professionals are often the torchbearers of discovery within the organization. They serve as advocates for continual employee growth and development. They are the experts in the field. They follow trends and bring knowledge and wisdom into the organization about employees and how to motivate them. They often serve as counselors or coaches for employees all levels. They provide insight about potential career paths and growth opportunities.

The individual employee, however, has ultimate responsibility for Discovering in organizations. Sitting on one's heels and waiting for the boss to come and lay out the future is a sure prescription for failure. A common lament from people we have talked to is that they thought that the organization would take care of them and their future. They were sorely disappointed as more proactive coworkers set career goals, worked to achieve them, and moved ahead. Each individual's aspirations reside inside. The organization can facilitate Discovering, but each person has to take command of her or his own future dreams.

Benefits of Discovering Process

For individuals, the benefits of discovering passion are obvious. Knowing what you love to do and want to do in the future begins to put you in charge of your life. Knowing what you love and want to do is an organizing mechanism—it provides a context around which all of your life decisions can be made. Knowing what you love and want to do gives hope. Knowing what you love and want to do begins the process of unleashing your own personal power.

For organizations, the benefits of discovering passion are twofold. First, supporting employee Discovering provides the means to set free all of the talent residing within. Employees will more likely be doing work they love to do. The effect is synergistic as passion from one quarter builds on that from another. The practical result—more productivity. The qualitative result—more enjoyment working there. Second, knowing and being clear about what the organization is passionate about doing will draw the kind of talented employees the organization needs and will make it more likely that they will be retained. Having a moving vision and mission and inspirational leadership are essential to talent recruitment and retention.

Unless a person has been passionate and lost that passion it's hard to understand how transitory passionate work can be and how difficult it can be to find it in the first place. One twenty-four-year-old teacher told us that although she had been passionate about chemistry in high school and was sure that her calling was to be a teacher, she has never had passion for teaching. Another person, a student in his thirties, described his situation:

I entered my 30s in a state of confusion, mixed with a smattering of longing. Old habits, interests, and pleasures no longer sustained me. My idealistic outlook failed to feed my imagination. I didn't know it then, but it was time to begin peeling away the first layers of life's illusions. I began to question without knowing how, who I was, and what life was for. It seemed I had no guidelines or energy to create. Simply living day-to-day, working 9 to 5, led nowhere. If I'd been asked to rate my life on a scale of one to ten, I'd have answered, what scale? The road I was wandering led nowhere.

One thing is clear; a person who doesn't have a goal will be used by someone who does. Likewise, a person who doesn't have passion of his own will get sucked into the passion of others, for better or worse. As John Sculley, former CEO of Apple Computer, said, "The new corporate contract is that we'll offer you an opportunity to express yourself and grow, if you promise to leash yourself to our dream, at least for awhile" (Whyte 1994: 78). Successful companies demand conformance to their passionate cultures, even if the culture itself encourages risk taking, as Collins and Porras (1997) found in their study of visionary companies.

During a research team meeting, one of our research assistants made the observation, "Joining these companies reminds me of joining an extremely tight-knit group or society. And if you don't fit, you'd better not join. If you're willing to really buy in and dedicate yourself to what the company stands for, then you'll be very satisfied and productive—probably couldn't be happier. If not, however, you'll probably flounder, feel miserable and out-of-place, and eventually leave—ejected like a virus. It's binary: You're either in or you're out, and there seems to be no middle ground. It's almost cult-like." (122)

One person gave us a concrete example. "Since I had no passion of my own, I got married and made my husband's passion for the air force my passion. I had totally denied myself of my own passion."

Discovering—Enablers

Discovering involves finding the kind of work that a person can be fervent about doing either in the short or long term. There are five enablers that facilitate the Discovering process. These are all interrelated, but are described separately for emphasis. Each of these elements can be practiced by individuals or provided by organizations to employees. Organizations, through normal personal development planning or special career development planning programs, can facilitate Discovering processes for employees.

Learning for Individuals

Discovering, by its very nature, is a learning process. Situations that facilitate learning new things, in new ways, with new people, and new perspectives, facilitate the discovery process. Going back to school is often a venue for the Discovering process, as Steve Preskill, a writer and professor, told us.

> No, I know exactly when it started. It started in graduate school. It started when I was in the University of Illinois in the early 80s studying history and philosophy of education and other things related to that. And realizing that my love for education and my love for history were being combined in some wonderful ways that I had never even imagined were possible before.

Learning is a key to discovering what is most meaningful to us. In *Effective Teaching and Mentoring: Realizing the Transformational Power of Adult Learning Experiences,* Laurent Daloz said, "A good education tends to our deepest parts, enriches them, nourishes the questions from which grow the tentative answers that, in turn, sow fresh questions about what is important" (1986: 2).

Learning also occurs vicariously. We learn by watching others, observing them in action. Find a mentor or someone who does what you think might be passionate work. Follow them. Listen to their advice. Learn from them. Personal coaches can also be helpful in providing advice, perspective, and feedback.

We will return to learning again. It is the most fundamental source of passionate work, and we look at it from a variety of perspectives.

Learning for Organizations

In organizations that promote learning, Discovering is a natural way of life. Individuals are called upon to test tacit assumptions about the organization and its future. Employees are encouraged to develop a personal vision of their future and are supported in developing skills and knowledge to create that future.

Senge, Kleiner, Roberts, Ross, and Smith describe the five "disciplines" of learning organizations. One discipline, Personal Mastery, involves setting up the conditions that encourage and support people who want to increase their own abilities. Personal Mastery necessitates "articulating a personal vision, seeing current reality clearly, and choosing: making a commitment to creating the results you want" (1994: 195). Senge asks his readers to imagine what an organization can expect from the practice of personal mastery.

> Imagine an organization full of people who come to work enthusiastically, knowing that they will grow and flourish, and intent on fulfilling the vision and goals of the larger organization. There's an ease, grace, and effortlessness about the way they get things done. Work flows seamlessly among teams and functions. People take pleasure and pride in every aspect of the enterprise—for example, in the way they can talk openly, reflect on each other's opinions, and have genuine influence on the structures around them. That's a lot of energy walking in each day, accomplishing an ever-increasing amount of work and having fun along the way. (198)

Organizations, Senge says, must invest the time, energy, and money necessary to provide conditions in which "individuals can develop their capacity to create what they care about . . . " (199). Working with Personal Mastery, he says, means entering into matters of the heart. "Developing a personal vision means tapping into a deep well of hope and aspiration." (199).

This visioning process is a Discovering process. Organizations that promote learning in all of its guises—action learning, formal learning, developmental and career planning, incidental learning—create the conditions for self-introspection and experimentation that facilitate Discovering.

Experimenting/Changing for Individuals

People get snookered into thinking that what they have is the best thing that they could hope for. One way to discover what you love to do is to try things. Those attempts might be small and of little risk, like volunteering for a community organization or taking dance lessons, or they could be major, like changing jobs or careers. Sometimes it just involves taking a chance and seeing all the pieces fall into place, as a co-owner of a kaleidoscope store told us.

> We kind of stumbled upon it. It was one of those flukes where two lives come together at the same time and you're thinking the same kind of thoughts. And Pat wanted to open a business and I had no idea I would ever want to open a business, especially in kaleidoscopes. But, she collected them and I was wanting to make them. So together, it just happened. It was meant to be.

When people think about their futures and what would make them passionate they sometime balk. "What if this isn't the right choice?" they worry. They paralyze themselves by thinking that there is only one answer. In fact, there may be many answers or many combinations of answers, which can only be discerned by trying things out.

Sometimes Discovering just takes getting out and doing things. In *The Intimate Choreographer,* Blom and Chaplin say discovering in their world happens as it happens. "The choreographer goes to the studio and begins to work, and in the working, in the moving, something happens, something connects, something becomes important, and almost on their own, the theme and intention self-clarify" (1982: 9).

Experimenting/Changing for Organizations

Corporations are no different. Sometimes it just takes getting out and doing things as an organization. Collins and Porras say:

> It makes no sense to analyze whether an envisioned future is the "right" one. With a creation—and the task is to create a future, not to predict the future—there can be no right answer. Did Beethoven create the "right" Ninth Symphony? Did Shakespeare create the "right" Hamlet? We can't answer these questions, they're nonsense. The essential questions about the envisioned future involve such questions as: "Does it get our juices flowing? Do we find it stimulating? Does it stimulate forward momentum? Does it get people going?" (1997: 235)

Organizations can provide many opportunities for experimentation and change. Job rotations, special assignments, and community leadership positions are all opportunities to give employees new ways of looking at organizational work. Boredom is one of the great passion-reducers, so change in itself can be good. When used to help an employee explore venues for passionate work, experimentation can be even more powerful. The caveat, of course, is that change can be scary and new assignments inevitably reduce proficiency and productivity for a period of time. Therefore, providing a supportive environment will be essential to reap both the organizational and individual benefits of planned experimentation. An added organizational benefit will be the development of a more flexible, wiser workforce.

Meditating/Reflecting for Individuals

Reflection is intentionally thinking about what works or doesn't work, what has been exciting, used to be exciting, isn't exciting anymore, or what could be exciting. Reflection at its best is thinking about possibilities and assumptions that are normally never explored. It's asking "what if" questions regularly. These "what if" questions might seem almost sacrilegious or macabre but they are fundamental to discovery. Here, for example, are some "what if" questions:

What (would I do), if:

> I got fired tomorrow?
> I developed a serious health problem?
> The company merged with another one sometime in the next six months?
> I approached my job completely differently?
> I (or my spouse) decided to go back to school?

What (could I do), if:

> I decided that I wanted to travel more/less?
> I quit my job tomorrow?
> I set a five-year target? How could I make it come true?
> My spouse and I got excellent jobs on separate coasts?

One professional in her twenties told us that she had lost her passion but found it again "primarily by stepping back and reflecting upon a particular time or event in my life that led to that passion."

Contemplation is something we talk about but then, too often, forgo. Yet it is invaluable for uncovering the deepest understanding of yourself. Rilke, writing at the turn of the nineteenth century, advised a young poet to reflect deeply.

> You are looking outside, and that is what you should most avoid right now. No one can advise or help you—no one. There is only one thing you should do. Go into yourself. Find out the reason that commands you to write; see whether it has spread its roots into the very depths of your heart; confess to yourself whether you would have to die if you were forbidden to write. This most of all: ask yourself in the most silent hour of your night: *must* I write. Dig into yourself for a deep answer. And if this answer rings out in assent; if you meet this solemn question with a strong, simple "*I must*," then build your whole life in accordance with this necessity; your whole life, even into its humblest and most indifferent hour, must become a sign and witness to this impulse. (1984: 5–6)

In *The Skillful Teacher*, Stephen Brookfield advises, "So if you have forgotten what inspired you to become a teacher in the first place, and if you can't recall why you felt it was such an important way to spend your life, make a deliberate and repeated effort to revisit the source of your decisions and to drink from the waters there" (1990: 28).

Meditating/Reflecting for Organizations

The annual process for creating personal development plans is a natural place for organizations to encourage reflection on career goals and opportunities. Immediate supervisors either repress or support this process. Selfish supervisors wanting to hold on to valuable employees may inhibit true employee reflection and try to keep workers tied to current jobs (and to assumptions about what their career potential is). Excellent supervisors encourage employee development, growth, and reflection. These supervisors attract the best and the brightest employees.

Career assessment centers are another natural place for employees to reflect on their future with the company or even for some other company. The danger of losing talented employees by encouraging them to think broadly about their careers is far less than the danger of having unhappy, nonproductive employees who feel captured by the company. The best people will leave anyway and the folks who stay behind will resent the organization.

Organizations can embed reflection into their own processes. In that way, organizations themselves develop a deeper understanding of their current situation and future. According to Hamel and Prahalad, "What prevents companies from creating the future is an installed base of thinking—the unquestioned conventions, the myopic view of opportunities and threats, and the unchallenged precedents that comprise the existing managerial frame" (1996: 66). The responsibility to reflect starts with the senior management team, but really permeates the entire organization. Strategic planning is really a focused, intentional organizational reflection process. Strategic planning makes tacit assumptions about the future explicit, tests them, and revises them; sets goals for the future based on the anticipated future; and then develops strategies to accomplish them.

Organizations also institutionalize reflection processes when they regularly conduct postmortems. Postmortems take a project and study it to see what can be learned from it—good or bad. This reflection process is more difficult in one sense—people may be defensive about what didn't go well and try to cover it up. When done in the spirit of learning of trying to avoid similar mistakes in the future, and of sharing knowledge, postmortems are an excellent source of organizational reflection.

Self-Awareness/Assessing for Individuals

One of the saddest stories people tell us is that, after blank (five, ten, twenty, . . .) years, they woke up and realized how miserable their career had been. In our workshops people often experience a series of emotions as they truly assess their lives. Self-awareness is the first step to passionate work, and it requires constant vigilance. It is easy to go through a day, a week, a year, or even five years without thinking too much about what makes life exciting. Often there's an underlying angst or unhappiness or even simply a feeling of survival until (fill one in): _____five o'clock _____ Friday _____retirement. Just "getting by" doesn't have anything to do with passionate work.

Assessment can be more formal. Use of 360-degree feedback can be illuminating. Career inventories can raise awareness. Assessment tools are plentiful and are available either in hard copy, on-line, or through career counseling. Asking a mentor or a coach to observe and report can also be helpful.

Self-Awareness/Assessing for Organizations

Organizations that want to facilitate introspection and thoughtful employee self-evaluations will provide opportunities either regularly or at least annually for employees to look at where they stand careerwise. Self-awareness also comes from thoughtful performance appraisal processes and supervisor coaching.

Organizations should also regularly assess themselves. Almost every organization has unspoken weaknesses or threats that no one will bring up. It helps from time to time to have someone from outside the organization conduct these evaluations.

Imagining for Individuals

Imagination is the portal to an intentional future. If you can imagine something and can clearly envision it, then it is possible to see the steps required to achieve your goal. Every person has the capacity to imagine. "The potential power of creative imagination is all but limitless," (Osborn 1963: 1). According to Mezirow (2000), "Imagination is central to understanding the unknown; it is the way we examine alternative interpretations of our experience by 'trying on' another's point of view. The more reflective and open we are to the perspectives of others, the richer our imagination of alternative contexts for understanding will be" (20). Without using our innate ability to envision what doesn't currently exist in our own experience we hamstring our ability to forge a desired future.

To create something—unless you want to depend on blind luck—it first has to be visualized. Try looking at the unusual. Read science fiction, look at historical figures you admire, mythology, think of your role models. Practice daydreaming. Place yourself in different, perhaps outlandish situations.

Try scenario planning, like major corporations do. Scenario planning is looking at several different potential futures and playing out possibilities and consequences. Making a commitment to a path is easier with a richer understanding of what might lie ahead in any direction.

In Chapter 4 we discussed Leider and Shapiro's (1995) definition of the perfect job. Imagine what that perfect job would be for you. What would you be doing? Who would you be doing it with? Where would you be? What would you be accomplishing? What would another perfect job for you be?

Individuals can call on professional organizations to ask themselves questions about the future. What will an accountant's office look like twenty years from now? How will a plumber be using technology to make the craft more effective? What will the tools of the trade be? How will teachers be teaching? Will they even have to leave their homes?

Imagining for Organizations

The imagining process for an individual is similar to organizational strategic visioning processes. Scanning the environment, looking at trends, emerging jobs and technology, the restructuring of economic institutions, picturing the future vividly, and what it might look like in detail are all closely related to what either an individual or an organization might do to imagine the future. Organizations can help individuals imagine their own potential futures by including them when looking at the future of the company or their industry. Successful organizations will be analyzing workforce trends and thinking about future job requirements. Ask your employees to look at trends in their own crafts or professions. Include them in workforce planning discussions. Engage them in visualizing the kinds of work that your organization will be doing and the kind of workers that will be needed.

The elements that facilitate the Discovery process are Learning, Experimenting/Change, Meditating/Reflecting, Self-Awareness/Assess-

TABLE 5.1   Discovering Enablers

	Activities
Learning	• Education/school • Observing others/mentoring • Personal coaching
Experimenting/change	• Job rotations • Special assignments • Community volunteering
Meditating/reflecting	• Reflection upon beliefs/assumptions • Asking "what if" questions • Personal development planning
Self-awareness assessment	• 360-degree feedback • Vocational assessments/aptitude tests • Performance appraisal • Career inventories
Imagination	• Visioning • Visualization • Scenario development

ing, and Imagining. These elements interact with each other and are essential to discovering a desired future (see Table 5.1).

Why Don't We Discover?

If Discovering is so important, why don't people do it? There are three main reasons.

Security—Individuals

It is a whole lot easier to continue with the tried and true. Security might lie in doing things in comfortable ways. Security might lie in safe relationships. Security might lie in having a predictable source of income and a plan for retirement. There is nothing inherently wrong with seeking security—unless it becomes an excuse for living unhappy lives. Lucas (1999), says "Money—or rather, what it represents to us in terms of material needs, desires, freedom and choice—is one other main reason why people shackle themselves to a job they detest. That, and never having taken the time or effort to discover what it is they really want to do for a living" (116). Although some people do find passion in the act of pursuing money, generally the acquisition of money is a necessary evil so that people can do what they really want to do.

Money and what it can buy is not, however, the only security crutch people lean on to avoid discovery. Many times security lies in being comfortable in the job and the people you work with.

Security—Organizations

Organizations are like individuals. They develop norms of behavior. They push everyone toward the center of an invisible normal distribution curve. They reject uniqueness. They discourage people who put the organization at risk. Organizations tout risk-taking but the tacit rules often have to do with sticking with the tried and true.

Learned Helplessness—Individuals

Learned helplessness is "the giving-up reaction, the quitting response that follows from the belief that whatever you do doesn't matter" (Seligman 1998: 15). Society can suppress the natural human tendency to learn and discover. Mom and Dad tell us not to follow our dream of becoming a poet because there's no money in it. A teacher tells us that we ought to think about becoming a teacher and not a mechanic (or vice versa) because we don't really have the talent to do one or the other. After a while we self-censor our dreams. Society doesn't have to do it for us anymore. It is frightening to think that society censors the dreams of whole classes of people before they even graduate from high school, and often many years before that. People with learned helplessness don't even try anymore. They take the first thing that comes along and say to themselves, "That's enough. I'll find my excitement in Sunday football games or my hobby."

Learned Helplessness—Organizations

Organizations often promote learned helplessness in their employees. Tacit understandings about who will and will not succeed tell employees in sometimes subtle ways that no matter how hard they try they can only go so far. There may be unspoken rules, for example, about what the ceiling is for a person without a college degree. Sooner or later these cause people to seek avenues for success outside the company or to just give up. Policies, procedures, and reward systems that stifle initiative may create an employee population that simply gives up.

Ignorance—Individuals

Ignorance is an ugly word. It implies something that's not true—ignorance does not mean lack of intelligence. In fact, every single one of us is ignorant in areas too numerous to count. For many, ignorance comes in two forms. The first is ignorance of one's own unhappiness. The second is ignorance about opportunities for passionate work.

Too many people don't even know enough about themselves to recognize that they're unhappy. Call it "lives of quiet desperation" or call it simple avoidance. Sometimes parents tell their children that life is not a bowl of cherries. The children resign themselves to unhappiness thinking that that's the way it's supposed to be. In any case, these folks don't seek to discover passionate work because they are simply unaware that life doesn't have to be a treadmill.

The other case of ignorance relates to opportunity. Many people don't explore because they don't know how to explore or even where to look. Like the adventurers of history, simply recognizing terra incognita and the possibility of finding undiscovered opportunities is enough to spur the discovery process.

Ignorance—Organizations

Every organization has a set of unwritten assumptions about the past, present, and future. Like every paradigm, these assumptions are often considered valid even when the environment changes. Much of strategic thinking involves testing assumptions about the future. Hamel and Prahalad say that "Companies that create the future are rebels. They're subversives. They break the rules. They're filled with people who take the other side of an issue just to spark a debate" (1994: 107). They are "contrarians" (107). That way they are prepared when the environment changes and avoid outdated beliefs that could cause organizational actions leading to disaster.

To the extent organizations reinforce unhealthy assumptions about the workforce itself, they inhibit growth. Stereotypes that promote success for one type of employee over another perpetuate conditions that are debilitating. Surfacing unspoken assumptions is a way of overcoming ignorance about how people are treated the way they are, and why. One of the most liberating acts is to create a climate in which critical thinking is the norm. Paulo Friere says that "Liberation is a praxis: the action and reflection of men and women upon their world in order to transform it" (1993: 60). Organizations often don't inform employees about their potential career paths, or even about the company's future direction. Ignorance stifles passionate work. Knowledge, dialogue, honesty, and a good healthy streak of contrarianism leads to engagement, commitment, and trust.

The Elements of Discovering

Every person has to decide what makes work passionate for him or her. Each person is different. One person loves the applause, another producing something that will transcend his life. Still another, making something that can be used today. Here are some ideas to keep in mind as you consider the work you would love to pursue.

Joy/Enthusiasm/Desire

What do you love to do more than anything? What makes you laugh out loud? What makes you smile when you think about doing it? A twenty-five-year-old retail manager says she is "passionate about my current job. I train people to make their customers' day by being friendly, helpful, understanding, tolerant, and genuine. . . . I absolutely live for customer satisfaction."

Steve Preskill, author and professor, describes the feeling as, "There's something in my stomach . . . there's something that happens in my stomach when I'm joyful that I can't explain. Some kind of—it's not a queasy feeling, but there's a swirling, overwhelming feeling of happiness, of this can't be true, but I can't quite put my finger on, but it's almost dizzying."

Parker Palmer, author of *The Courage to Teach,* says,

> I am a teacher at heart, and there are moments in the classroom when I can hardly hold the joy. When my students and I discover uncharted territory to explore, when the pathway out of a thicket opens up before us, when our experience is illumined by the lightening-life of the mind—then teaching is the finest work I know. (1998: 1)

In his book *The Reinvention of Work,* Matthew Fox says "We have a right to and a need for joy in our work" (95). Joy is an essential part of passionate work. What makes you joyous? What is so much fun to do that you can hardly stand it?

What can your organization do to make work more fun and exciting? Sometimes the work itself can only be made so interesting. In that case, how can you manage other elements—celebrations of success, parties, work games, and so on—to make work joyful? Some people respond to competition, some to creativity, some to continuous improvement, some to the relationships—the enjoyment of enjoyable people, some to the joy of success. Your job is to find those keys to enthusiasm locked inside your employees and inherent within the work itself and to unlock them.

Purpose/Meaning

Doing something significant is part of creating sustainable passion. Sometimes the situation is made significant simply by setting a goal or making a small wager on a golf match, which increases competitiveness. Sometimes a person doing something symbolic for her lover, giving a card or a small gift, makes an everyday situation meaningful. Sometimes a job that seemed boring or unimportant is made significant because a customer expresses appreciation for a small act of service. Finding the meaning and purpose in existing work or finding different work that is meaningful is critical for passionate work. What is meaningful for you?

A twenty-eight-year-old U.S. Air Force survivability analyst said, "I really got into managing the database. I was excited at the thought of what I could do to contribute to the defense of the country." A twenty-nine-year-old youth program coordinator found meaning in a different place. "Throughout high school, college, and just after graduation I was passionate about politics. That led to other community-based work, for which I had a passion. The lesson I learned was that my passion was not for government and politics, but the pursuit of social justice and change." A museum administrator told us "It was hard to make anything happen, but once I learned to operate within our budget and coordinate successful fundraisers I felt that there was hope. I found a new passion in making our museum a self-supporting department within the university." Each person has a different, unique sense of what is meaningful to her or him.

Perhaps the most important thing organizations can do to create overall purpose and meaning is to have powerful mission and vision statements. Organizations must have a deep sense of what they contribute to humanity. They must have a compelling view of the future. Effective leaders then communicate these to employees and make sure that each person knows how she or he is contributing to making a difference in society or to customers or to the organizational "family." Think of stories, movies, or real situations when a leader walked into an employee's office and said, "We need you," and why. The worker suddenly realized how important he or she was to the group. The task became meaningful. The worst thing, of course, that a supervisor can do is to overtly or covertly insinuate that the employee is just a cog and easily replaceable.

Genuineness

Ask yourself the question, Who am I really? Who is the real me? When all is said and done, to be happy you have to be yourself. Some people never find themselves because they aren't willing to take the risk of digging beneath the surface. They are satisfied with living less-than. Having cast your net wide to look outside and inside, the last question is, "Who am I?" What do I feel natural doing, what feels right?

In her book *Do What You Love: The Money Will Follow,* Marsha Sinetar described work that, for her, was not genuine.

Work I disliked the most was work I wasn't suited for. Once, for example, I sold vacuum cleaners door to door. Now there's nothing wrong with that job, except that I was painfully shy and basically introverted, and knocking on doors in strange neighborhoods was, for me, an unnatural act. But I was working my way through college and in desperate need of tuition money, so I silenced my fears and told myself I could do it. The money was good, and that somehow made it all right. The only catch was my heart wasn't in it. I lasted one day. Looking back on that experience and others depressingly like it, I realized that I am not cut out for some occupations. I have a specific disposition and a given set of aptitudes that require an equally specific type of work. I know now that work needs to fit my personality just as shoes need to fit my feet. (7)

Women have told us how difficult it was being genuine in male-dominated organizations. Barbara Grogan, the president of a millwrighting firm, was interviewed in Sally Helgeson's *The Female Advantage:*

Women have a mission to humanize the workplace by expressing their love, joy, enthusiasm, and caring. And we can't do that unless we are *ourselves.* I made the decision after I started my company that the only way I could succeed and have any fun was by being myself to the hilt. I knew I couldn't be one of those women in a dull suit with a little tie, trying to restrain my personality. (1990: 112–113)

A department head of a natural foods cooperative told us that the key to her passion was "living with the natural flows of my life, knowing myself well enough to keep plugging away at the things I love and value the most." A forty-year-old computer trainer told us her key to passion was to find a job that "harnessed my strengths. I love organization and I love imparting knowledge to others of my age group."

Being you. Being genuine. Knowing who you are and what is natural and right for you is essential.

Organizations have the primary responsibility for providing climates where individuals can feel natural and genuine. The key for successful organizations is to be intentional about what kinds of employees they want and to then create the climate where they can thrive. Every organization is not designed for every person. In fact, the strongest organizations will be the clearest about what behaviors (and therefore what kinds of individuals) are most valued, which makes it easy for an individual to see if they will have to fake it or can be genuine.

Remember, joy without meaning is superficial. Meaningfulness without joy is mere duty and responsibility. Perhaps most important is genuineness, being who you really are.

Transformation Theory

The theory and process that best describes the way individuals discover passionate work is transformation theory and the perspective transformation process. The person most intimately identified with these concepts is Jack Mezirow.

Transformation theory is well known to adult learning practitioners. It is one of the leading adult learning theories today, and though it has been elaborated upon and made richer it has stood the test of time. Currently, transformation theory is being applied in increasingly diverse settings to help adults develop broader, more useful, more healthy belief systems about themselves and the world. How transformation theory applies to passionate work, both descriptively and prescriptively, is the crux of this section.

Transformation theory attempts to explain the process wherein adults develop more dependable beliefs about their experience. Foundational to this is the process of becoming aware of one's own assumptions, which are often unspoken and even subconscious, as well as the assumptions of others, so that they can be examined, updated, rejected, or revised (Mezirow 2000).

Earlier in this chapter, we identified Discovering as occurring through two processes—intentional and imposed. Mezirow says that learning may be intentional, incidental, or assimilative (2000). Discovering, as discussed above, can be incremental, that is, evolutionary, as a person learns more and more about a particular task or job; or revolutionary, a quantum leap in self-understanding, as a person "sees the light" suddenly and significantly. Transformation theory suggests that transformations in our frames of reference, or paradigms, can be incremental, which involve a progressive series of transformations in points of view; or epochal, "a sudden, dramatic, reorienting insight . . . " (21).

Our points of view or habits of mind or frames of reference, each of which Mezirow defines a bit differently, are all based on the set of assumptions that we have about the world. They represent our beliefs, opinions, judgments, and understandings about the world. These assumptions were often created in our minds when we were young and continue to remain with us as adults even if they are not useful to us anymore. What are these assumptions or sets of assumptions, and why are they so important?

Table 5.2 notes Mezirow's Habits of Mind. For each of his habits we have added a corresponding set of questions. Each question is intended to help you begin the reflection process for that habit and the assumptions that underlie it. Many of these assumptions go unquestioned for a lifetime, or at least since the day someone—a coach, parent, teacher, or minister—told you not to question them. There are many more questions you can ask yourself. These are just starting points. Ask yourself lots and lots of questions and ask yourself why you believe the way you do.

Each one of these beliefs is an assumption you have about the world, which may or may not change depending on your circumstances and what you learn about yourself and the world. You are acting on that set of assumptions about yourself every minute, even if you aren't aware of what they are. The assumptions that you have about the world have more or less validity or have differing validity even depending on whose eyes they are being viewed from. Your belief may be considered "truth" when it is actually a locked-in assumption that has never been tested by enlarging your experience, your knowledge of the world, your range of relationships, or your own imagination. Whole groups of people, usually by an early age, limit their career aspirations because of assumptions that are derived from societal expectations and norms and internalized. Those assumptions are usually never tested—they are usually tacit or unconscious—and so restrictive that career decisions are made without even exploring potential sources of passionate work.

Every person carries assumptions in all of these areas that are either helpful or limiting. Any time you believe that you know the "truth," watch out. That is the time to test your thinking, to look at your belief in

TABLE 5.2   Habits of Mind

A set of assumptions that acts as a filter for interpreting the meaning of experience

Habit of Mind	Sample Questions to Test Your Assumptions
Sociolinguistic	• What do you believe to be true about other races? • What do you believe to be true about the opposite gender? Your own gender? • What "truths" do you believe about democracy, capitalism, feminism, and ageism? • When you speak of oppression, what are you assuming to be true? • What do you believe about sexuality, marriage? Why? • What do you believe to be important work? Is there work that is "above you"? "Below you"? Why?
Moral-ethical	• What do you believe to be moral? Amoral? Why? • What do you feel guilty about? • On what basis do you make ethical decisions? Why?
Epistemic	• Is there a best learning style? Why do you think that? • Do you count on the concrete or rely upon the abstract? Why?
Philosophical	• Do you believe in one god, several gods, or no god? • Is god a separate being, or a part of everything? • Does god have a gender? If so, what is it? • Do you believe humans are basically good? Bad? • Are you born with a god-given vocation?
Psychological	• Do you believe you are basically a good person? Bad person? • Do you believe you are talented? Why or why not? • What things did your parents tell you about yourself or your family or your heritage or your ethnicity that you still believe today? • Are you smart? Why do you think that?
Aesthetic	• What is beautiful? What is ugly? Why? • What are your criteria for beauty? Does anyone disagree with you? Why are they right/wrong? • What makes things funny or sad?

SOURCE: Adapted from Mezirow 2000.

different ways, to try to see it from another's perspective. If, having critically reflected on this belief and discovered it to be more valid than other competing or differing beliefs, then retain it provisionally as useful for your life. But retain it tentatively, so that you can always challenge it, try to understand it more deeply, and allow yourself to let it go if you find it's not useful anymore.

Wise people have deep sets of understandings about the world that they have developed by questioning them, by trying to understand them from multiple perspectives, and by listening to them being tested by others. Superficial people take the word of other "experts" as truth. These experts may indeed be wise or, perhaps more often, may be perceived as experts because they happen to be on television, are celebrities, or because they happen to be in a position of authority. Teachers, coaches, parents, ministers, and the like fit into this last category. Each of them can help you to understand the world, but adults must think critically about what they learn from others. Beware anyone claiming to know "the answer" or "the truth." Listen and learn most from people who qualify their own knowledge by providing other perspectives.

It is difficult for most people to challenge their own beliefs about the world. Many are used to depending on received knowledge, which is provided (most of the time unsolicited!) by someone else. Instead of critically thinking for ourselves we let others do it for us. When we do start thinking, our safe little world becomes tenuous and things we thought were written in stone become uncertain. Going to college often does that for people because they are forced to think about things, to associate with people, and to be exposed to ideas or ways of doing things that they hadn't before. Becoming immersed in different cultures can also have the same effect. For many people, this questioning of beliefs happens when we lose something that we thought we'd have forever— our marriage, a loved one, a job, or our health. When we start asking ourselves questions like "Is there really a God?" "Why am I here on earth?" and "What am I doing with my life?" we can tell that things we believed were "truth" about the world are open for questioning.

The discovery of passionate work for individuals is limited to the extent that they are unwilling to test their assumptions about what they can or cannot be or do, and is expanded to the extent they are willing to question their tried and true beliefs about themselves.

This questioning process begins with what Mezirow calls a "disorienting dilemma." The phases he describes are as follows:

1. A disorienting dilemma
2. Self-examination with feelings of fear, anger, guilt, or shame
3. A critical assessment of assumptions
4. Recognition that one's discontent and the process of transformation are shared
5. Exploration of options for new roles, relationships, and actions
6. Planning a course of action
7. Acquiring knowledge and skills for implementing one's plans
8. Provisional trying of new roles
9. Building competence and self-confidence in new roles and relationships
10. Reintegration into one's life on the basis of conditions dictated by one's new perspective. (2000: 22)

Mezirow calls this process Perspective Transformation, which results in a change in our frame of reference, which is the set of assumptions and expectations through which we filter and make sense of the world (Taylor, in Mezirow 2000).

Our Passion Transformation Model uses transformational learning as the major source of change. Steps 1–5 are analogous to our Discovery process, Step 6 to our Designing process, and Steps 7–10 to our Developing process.

Disorienting dilemmas are typically described as being triggered by a significant personal event. However, the triggering process can be much more complex than this, and can involve "integrating circumstances" (Taylor, in Mezirow 2000: 299) which are not sudden but are more cumulative of individual experiences which "provide an opportunity for exploration and clarification of past experiences" (299). Triggering events can be cumulative, with perhaps a catalytic event that triggers a perspective transformation, or perhaps not. They can be major and traumatic or relatively minor. This is akin to the evolutionary and revolutionary discovery processes described above.

Transformation has both cognitive and affective components. It involves looking at things in new ways and the feelings that are associated with potential and real loss or anticipated gain. Discovering passionate work entails both as well. Critically reflecting upon what you love to do, what is holding you back, what is meaningful work, what scares you, what you always wished to do but never thought you were right for, what you would sacrifice for, and so on all involve emotions. We often do not explore because we are afraid of what we might find. Transformation theory suggests that new perspectives are triggered by something that causes us to look at ourselves, to question ourselves, to deal with our emotions, and to assess what we believe in.

Kroth and Boverie (2000) found that the transformational learning process can cause adults to revise or to reinforce the set of assumptions that they carry about their life purpose or direction. The relationships and process are shown in the Life Mission and Adult Learning Model (Kroth and Boverie 2000: 144), Figure 5.1. Often, life mission is unknown or assumed, sometimes it is well known, but it changes because of either a single life-altering event (loss of job, for example), or through a series of events (new job assignments, changes in technology, or classwork, as examples), which cause the individual to reassess what she believes her life mission to be. This transformational process

FIGURE 5.1   Life Mission and Adult Learning Model

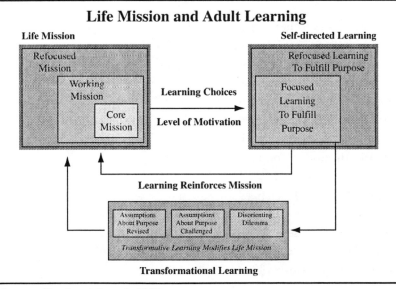

SOURCE: Kroth and Boverie 2000.

affects the individual's learning process, focusing it or refocusing it as assumptions change, increasing or decreasing self-directed learning depending on that focus, and continually reinforcing the assumed life mission until another disorienting dilemma transforms the assumptions again.

Summary

For organizations, putting time and effort into the Discovering process is one of those you-can-pay-me-now-or-pay-me-later propositions. Developing a strong sense of mission, vision, and corporate culture will help you choose the right employees in the first place, engage them in the work of the company, increase organizational trust and commitment, and make them more productive. Developing strong Discovering processes for employees will help them understand themselves, increase your ability to retain them, and provide focus for their career development process.

As you begin your discovery process, keep Steven Ambrose's description of Meriwether Lewis in your mind. In *Undaunted Courage,* Ambrose paints a clear picture of one of the world's most courageous discoverers as he and William Clark moved into uncharted territory.

> He was entering a heart of darkness. Deserts, mountains, great cataracts, warlike Indian tribes—he could not imagine them, because no American had ever seen them. But, far from causing apprehension or depression, the prospects brought out his fullest talents. . . . Lewis had come to the point that he longed for, worked for, dreamed of all his life. He was ready, intensely alive. . . . He had an endearing sense of wonder and awe at the marvels of nature that made him the nearly perfect man to be the first to describe the wonders of the American West.
>
> He turned his face west. He would not turn it around until he reached the Pacific Ocean. He stepped forward, into paradise. (216)

For some individuals, the Discovering process is the most difficult. A twenty-nine-year-old, just about to graduate from college, walks into his parents' dining room and wonders—both rhetorically and plaintively—

what he will do with his life after graduation. A woman in her fifties, about to retire after thirty years, asks herself what she will do with her life after she receives the gold watch. For others, finding passion is the easy part—living it is the hard part. Designing your life to achieve your passion is the second passion transformation process and is described in the next chapter.

There are many exercises for discovering passion or personal mission. We have given you a few simple ones to help you begin your Discovering process.

EXERCISE NINE: Discovering—Individual

Visualizing Your Passion
Sit with eyes closed in a quiet place.

Remember a time when you loved your work. It could be a single project, a particular part of a job, or the whole job. Try to visualize how you felt, what you were doing, the people around you, the way you felt about the work itself.

Now think about how you got into this particular situation. What led up to it. Visualize the process of moving toward that passionate work. Now think about why this passionate period or job ended. What happened? How did you feel? What were the causes?

Now picture yourself moving toward a new job or reworking your current job to make it more meaningful, more fun. What would have to happen? What would your workplace look like, feel like, sound like? Think about yourself. How are you different? How do you feel?

Now visualize an "ideal work day" five years from now.

___Where would you like to be working?

___With whom?

___What specifically would you like to be doing at work?

___How would you like to be feeling?

Now try to think carefully about the steps to reaching this new or better job.

EXERCISE TEN: Discovering—Individual

Your Passionate Job Description

Describe Your Passionate Work. Write a statement outlining what would be passionate work for you. What kind of job would make you feel passionate most of the time? What would the environment be like? The people? The work itself? What would you have to change or modify about yourself to be in this job?

Now ask yourself these questions about the passionate work you have described for yourself.

> Does your passionate job description inspire you?
>
> If you were to live your passion, would it inspire others?
>
> Would you wake up most mornings eager and delighted to do it?
>
> Would it keep you interested and energized even when others would give up or burn out?
>
> Would you occasionally find yourself enjoying what you do so much that you couldn't believe you're getting paid for it?
>
> Would you do it even if you didn't get paid?
>
> By carrying out your passionate work, would you provoke passion in other people?
>
> Would other people come to you to find out what your "secret" is?

Now inquire within. Are there assumptions that I have made about myself, or about my capabilities that could be keeping me from realizing my fullest potential?

Have I imposed any limits on myself? Where did these limits come from? Are they really valid?

What fears are keeping me from having a career where I find passionate work?

Do I blame other people, forces, or events for my current situation?

Do you have a purpose in life? Ask yourself why you are here on this earth. Does your passionate job description depict some special calling for your life?

If I fulfill the passionate job description I wrote above will I wake up most Mondays feeling energized because I'm doing important work?

Will I have deep energy to fulfill a personal calling for my work?

Will I be clear about how I measure my success as a person?

Will I be using my talents to add real value to people's lives?

Will I be working with people who honor the values I care about?

Does your passionate job description describe work that is delightful and fun?

Will I be making a living doing what I most love to do?

Will I feel free to speak my mind at work?

Will I experience true joy in my work?

Will there be days I laugh out loud because I am having so much fun?

EXERCISE ELEVEN: Discovering—Organizations

Organizations have two main arenas for consideration when it comes to the Discovering process. The first relates to discovering a passionate purpose for the organization itself; the second to how well the organization facilitates Discovering for its employees.

Discovering Organizational Passion
Describe your organization's mission and vision? Are they inspiring? Would the statements themselves heighten employee passion for work, or not?

If the mission and vision are inspiring, does the organization actually live them? Or are they just mottos on a wall? Would the way the organization follows the spirit of the mission and vision heighten employee passion for their work, or are the mission and vision perceived as hollow sentiments?

Are organizational leaders, in particular senior leaders, passionate about their work? Do the leaders themselves heighten employee passion for their work, or not?

Have senior leaders discovered how to link organizational mission and vision to employees' needs for fun and meaningful work?

Organizational Support for Employee Discovering
Is the organization passionate about helping employees find work that they are passionate about? Is it a burning priority? Is employee recruitment, development, and retention a strategic objective?

Is there a comprehensive career development program for employees at all levels? Are there individual career interest inventories and other assessments that engage employees in discovering what kind of work they would love to do?

Does the performance management system include a strong developmental emphasis? Are employees encouraged to grow and learn and to try differing job assignments?

Are managers and supervisors rewarded for developing their employees and penalized for viewing them as possessions?

Are there formal or informal mentoring programs available to employees who want to learn more about different aspects of the company, professional growth, or leadership?

The Designing Process **6**

Designing Process
Organization Individual

**Designing
Enabling Processes**

Goal
To develop and implement
strategies for living
discovered passion

But in discussing an approach to bringing about positive changes within oneself, learning is only the first step. There are other factors as well: conviction, determination, action, and effort. *So the next step is developing conviction.* Learning and education are important because they help one develop conviction of the need to change and help to increase one's commitment. *This conviction to change then develops into determination. Next, one transforms determination into action*—the strong determination to change enables one to make a sustained effort to implement the actual changes. *This final factor of effort is critical.*

—HH DALAI LAMA AND CUTLER 1998: 220

Designing

Jane Alexander's book, *Spirit of the Home: How to Make Your Home a Sanctuary,* describes the process for making a house a home. A home, Alexander says, "is far more than a physical structure; it is a living entity with a soul of its own. In the past the home was honored as a deity—it was considered to have its own spirit and a host of attending spirits" (1998: 2). She describes the art of homemaking, which consists of putting the heart into home, recognizing the home as a reflection of soul, understanding the psychology of the home, identifying your ideal home, and then ascertaining what is needed to have the "Clear, clean," the "Energetic," and the "Sensual" home. She talks about the home as a "Sanctuary for the Soul" and "How your home can bring love and romance."

Designing your life's work is analogous to designing a house. First, you have to visualize it (our *Discovery* process), then you have to draw up the plans (that's our *Designing* process), and finally you have to build it (our *Development* process). For organizations, Hamel and Prahalad call it "strategic architecture" (1994: 117). "Not only must the future be imagined," they say, "it must be built" (117).

> An architect must be capable of dreaming things not yet created—a cathedral where there is now only a dusty plain, or an elegant span across a chasm that hasn't yet been crossed. But an architect must also be capable of producing a blueprint for how to turn the dream into reality. An architect is both a dreamer and a draftsman. An architect marries art with structural engineering. (117)

Once a building is built it can be customized as your needs change. It can be remodeled if it becomes boring. Sometimes it is simply outgrown, or your life changes so much that you have to move to another house completely.

In the same way, you may either remodel your own work to make it passionate or you may need to find a completely new line of work or job so that you can work with joy and meaningfulness. If it is remodeling, you may be able to make simple, relatively small changes in your current work environment. If you've decided that a new career is required, however, then, like building your own home, it will take an investment in planning, time, and most likely the courage to do something uncharted.

Goal of the Designing Process

For individuals, the overarching goal of the designing process is to develop strategies to begin living your purpose. Part of the designing process includes all the preparations—mental, social, spiritual, physical—necessary to embark upon passionate work. As an individual, that includes planning strategically and practically how you will achieve the goal of passionate work. For organizations, the overarching goal of the designing process is to create a passionate work environment for your employees. For both individuals and organizations, the purpose is to be intentional and it is about creating the means to achieve passionate work.

The Designing process may feel natural, genuine, and effortless or it may feel unnatural. It may feel clumsy. It may be so scary that it is difficult to sleep at night. It may not be easy to fulfill. Moving from one place to another is often challenging. It takes new skills and perspectives. It may involve reorienting long-established relationships. It probably will require saying "no" to activities that have to date been a big part of your life and to people who demand unproductive time from you. As you draw up your plans for the future, as you acquire the underpinnings for what you are building, continually revisit your goal. Is it challenging enough? If it is too challenging for now, can you take it in bites? Although it is important to be realistic, try not to compromise because of obstacles that feel overwhelming. With enough time, many barriers can be overcome.

Transitions

Transitions are difficult. In *Transitions,* William Bridges says, "love relationships and work are the two important factors through which a person's inner changes become visible" (1980: 58). The impact of these changes, he says, is enormous. Careers go through phases and difficulty comes not only from learning about the new situation, but also from the process of letting go of the person you used to be and then finding the new person. Pursuing passionate work may require letting go of habits, activities, and relationships that don't serve you anymore. Bridges's book provides an excellent guide for anyone transitioning from one thing—job, relationship—to another. He provides a transition checklist for love and work, which is summarized here.

Love and Work: A Transition Checklist.

1. *Take your time.* Outer forms of our lives can change in an instant, but the inner reorientation takes time. You cannot rush the inner process.
2. *Arrange temporary structures.* You will need to work out ways of continuing with your life while the inner work is being done. This may involve getting a temporary job while you look for a real job; it may involve agreements at home or work to carry on in some modified fashion until something more permanent can be devised; or it may simply involve an inner resolve to accept a given situation as temporary.
3. *Don't act for the sake of action.* There is likely to be a temptation to "do something—anything." This reaction is understandable but it usually leads to more difficulty. The transition process requires not only that we bring a chapter of our lives to conclusion, but also that we discover whatever we need to learn for the next step we are going to take.
4. *Recognize why you are uncomfortable.* Distress is not necessarily a sign that something has gone wrong but that something is changing. It is essential to understand the transition process, to expect times of anxiety, to expect others to be threatened, and to expect old fears to be awakened.
5. *Take care of yourself in little ways.* Find the little continuities that are important when everything else seems to be changing.
6. *Explore the other side of the change.* If you have not chosen the change, there are a dozen reasons not to see its possible benefits. On the other hand, if you have chosen your change,

there are just as many reasons to avoid considering the price to be paid. In either case, explore the other side of the situation.

7. *Get someone to talk to.* It is just as important to have someone to simply listen to your dilemmas and your feelings as it is to get their advice.
8. *Find out what is waiting in the wings of your life.* There are unlived potentialities, interests, and talents within you that you have not explored. Recognize that transitions clear the ground for new growth.
9. *Use this transition as the impetus to a new kind of learning.* You knew what you needed to know to succeed in the past, but be aware that what you are going to become will require new understandings and new skills that you may not yet possess.
10. *Recognize that transition has a characteristic shape.* Things end, there is a time of fertile emptiness, and then things begin anew. (adapted from Bridges 1980: 78–82)

Transitions are difficult, and we are always transitioning from something to another thing. Indeed, we are always in the "process of becoming" (Rogers 1961: 196). We are, both as individuals and as organizations, works–in–progress.

One of our interviewees told us how she began to take the transitional steps that eventually led to her current passion for work.

In 1993, my spouse left a job in Wisconsin and took a job in Iowa. I followed him, leaving my job as a principal. But, I had a plan. I made a deal with my spouse that if I could sell our home in Wisconsin without a realtor I could take the commission and use it to fund an idea I had. I sold the house to the first person who came to see it.

So, armed with my $10,000 start up money, I developed a mail order catalog of artwork by women artists. The catalog was called "Seven Sisters." 10% of all sales went to *Y-ME*, a breast cancer organization in Chicago.

Organizational transitions can be traumatic. People tend to resist organizational change. Having another person's will imposed on us makes us push back. David Noer (1993), researching employees who had survived layoffs in their organization, found their feelings and concerns fell into fifteen categories:

> Job insecurity; unfairness; depression, stress, and fatigue; reduced risk taking and motivation; distrust and betrayal; optimism; continuing commitment; lack of reciprocal commitment; wanting it to be over; dissatisfaction with planning and communication; anger over the layoff process; lack of strategic direction; lack of management credibility; short-term profit orientation; sense of permanent change. (p. 54)

Transitioning in any instance is difficult. James O'Toole says that successful change efforts he studied had the following elements in common. Successful change:

1. had top management support;
2. built upon the organization's unique strengths and values;
3. did not have specifics imposed from the top;
4. was holistic; changing one part of the system required changing other parts;
5. was planned;
6. was made in the guts of the organization—including power relationships, access to information, and reward systems;
7. was approached from a stakeholder viewpoint, often coming from the external environment, from customers;
8. became ongoing.
   (Adapted from O'Toole 1996: 74–75)

We have divided this chapter into two major sections—one discussing designing for individuals and one discussing designing for organizations. In practice, however, there is considerable overlap between what individuals and organizations can do to design conditions that foster passionate work.

Designing for Individuals

Interior Design

When considering how to make your aspirations into reality, the first place to look is inside yourself. Have you designed a plan for yourself? Are you completely aware of your strengths and weaknesses—what will stop you from doing the passionate work you've identified? How about your personality? Do you have the fortitude and sense of personal power to stay the course, and the flexibility to adapt to changing circumstances? The emotional intelligence to lead your own life?

Sometimes the identification of passionate work is the hardest part for people. Sometimes, though, it's the next step, making it happen, aligning everything so that the vision can come true, and then having the will to carry it out, that's the most difficult.

Assessing.

> I've never done a single thing I've wanted to in my whole life! I don't know's I've accomplished anything except just get along. I figure I've made about a quarter of an inch out of a possible hundred rods. Well, maybe you'll carry things on further. I don't know. But I do get a kind of sneaking pleasure out of the fact that you knew what you wanted to do and did it. Well, those folks in there will try to bully you, and tame you down. Tell 'em to go to the devil! I'll back you. Take your factory job, if you want to. Don't be scared of the family. No, nor all of Zenith. Nor of yourself, the way I've been. Go ahead old man! The world is yours! [George Babbitt to his son] (Lewis 1996: 355)

Are you making a "quarter of an inch out of a possible hundred rods"? Do you know folks who are trying to "tame you down"? Bully you into working at things you don't want? What are your personal strengths, weaknesses, or matters of character that will allow you to succeed or to inevitably fail in your new endeavor? Are you strong enough to tell your organization "to go to the devil" when it trivializes your work or under-utilizes your creativity and talents? Personal assessment is a critical part of designing your future.

Take Responsibility for Your Life

The most important decision that you will make is to take full responsibility for your life. Over thirty years ago Rollo May wrote, "The tendency to see ourselves as the spawns of determinism has spread, in late decades, to include contemporary man's conviction that he is the helpless object of scientific forces in the form of atomic power" (1969: 184). Covey (1989) describes three sources of determinism—genetic, psychic, and environmental—that people often blame when they abdicate their power of choice. Peterson, Maier, and Seligman have studied learned helplessness and the importance of personal control. They say, "Other theorists had talked about control before, but work on learned helplessness has documented the importance of this variable in the broadest of terms—from biochemical to societal levels" (1993: 305). Whyte says, "If we can see the path ahead laid out for us, there is a good chance it is not our path; it is probably someone else's we have substituted for our own" (1994: 89), and "You can blame your mother, you can blame your father and *his* father for the problems with which you are destined to wrestle, but ultimately you are the one in whom they have made a home. You are the one who must say *Thus far and no farther,* and then go down and confront them yourself" (39). You know the goal, now the task is to lay out the path, *your* path, to get there and to have the willpower to take each step of the way.

We have spoken to employee after employee who blames everyone except the person most responsible—him or herself—for the circumstances of life. Personal choice is a quality only humans have. Other living beings in the world are directed in their actions by instinct. We cannot control everything that comes our way but we have complete control over how we choose to deal with those things.

Acknowledging that we alone are responsible for our lives is the first step to personal power. It is the key to success. Lacking that, we mire ourselves in what should have been, what could have been, and what would have been. The past, for example, is a great source of blame and self-victimization. Feelings of remorse, revenge, and sadness tie our hands in the present and may cause us to give up on the future. Freeing yourself from the past and instead taking responsibility for every action in the present is an essential part of taking control of your life. Acknowledge that you have choices. Make choices consistent with your goal. Act accordingly. Personal choice and volition are inextricably linked.

The easiest thing to do is set a challenging goal and then give every excuse in the world not to achieve it. There are many books about finding your vision and purpose—important books—but we find a dearth of material about developing the will to make and keep the decisions required for success. How well do you overcome obstacles? How persistent are you? Bleyl (2000) recently studied wisdom and wise people. Every wise person she studied had to overcome tremendous adversity. Have you developed habits of mind that give you the confidence and the determination to overcome obstacles? There will surely be barriers standing between you and passionate work. Do you have the volition to overcome them?

The development of will is like the exercise of a muscle. If your goal is to lose twenty pounds, the result will depend on countless decisions made over several months. To the extent you increasingly make choices to eat properly you are developing this muscle. To the extent you let circumstances make the choices for you (fast food right around the corner, let's see what's in the refrigerator, someone baked cookies, and so forth), then the muscle atrophies.

The same is true about achieving passionate work. If you relinquish your dream the first time someone says no or when you run into a conflict or if you run low on money or other resources or if you give up because it simply seems like it is taking forever, then you obviously will not make it. Sometimes people find unusual sources of will and character when emergencies draw out exceptional powers, but most of the time people with strong will have developed it over time, and it is then available to be called upon when needed. Developing this will requires making and keeping little decisions every day, and practicing doing what you say that you will do, so that your word to yourself is your bond. Doing something as simple as deciding to run around the block every day, and then making the choice every day to do it builds the will muscle. Making and keeping promises to yourself builds personal power, confidence, and satisfaction. Soon your word is your bond to yourself and to others.

Belenky, Clinchy, Goldberger, and Tarule use the metaphor of silence and voice to describe the process of developing personal agency. "We adopted the metaphor of voice and silence as our own. It has become a unifying theme that links the chapters in our story of women's ways of knowing and of the long journey they must make if they are to put the knower back into the known and claim the power of their own minds and voices" (1986: 19). They describe this journey of developing personal agency as moving from "silence" to "received knowledge" to "subjective knowledge" to "procedural knowledge" to "constructed knowledge" (15).

By developing the will, you develop agency, or personal power. Organizations can create conditions that facilitate employee empowerment, but the sources of personal power—will, intention, and action—reside within the individual. The stronger individual desire or motivation is, the more likely a person is to make decisions designed to achieve that desire. Expectancy theory suggests that the higher the expectation is that a certain action will result in a certain outcome, the higher the resulting motivation will be. The lower the expectation that a certain action will result in a certain outcome, the lower the resulting motivation.

How willing are you to stay the course? Although you may be able to identify your passionate work easily and begin pursuing it, financial or other success may prove elusive. Are you willing to work for its own sake? Writers, actors, singers, artists, entrepreneurs, and other people who follow their muse often do so by leaving security and income behind.

Skills/Knowledge/Competencies

Knowing the skills and knowledge you will need to acquire will be necessary, as well as an honest understanding of your current levels of expertise. The gap between required and current expertise represents your development plan. Successful people have a clear idea of what they need to do and learn to bridge the gap between dream and reality. Akin to the Discovering process, this kind of self-assessment looks not at what your passionate work should be but at what your abilities are to achieve the passionate work you have identified. Excellent vehicles to develop essential self-knowledge for your own assessment are to visit career counselors, take courses, ask experts to review your résumé, take 360 degree or other instruments, review performance appraisals, and seek advice from your supervisor or others you respect. There are many perspectives that can help you to determine where you stand, so we'll just mention key areas that sometimes are overlooked. One area that has received an enormous amount of attention recently is emotional intelligence.

Emotional Intelligence. Daniel Goleman (1998) found that 67 percent of the abilities that are important for effective performance are what he calls emotional competencies. This was true for all of the categories of jobs and the range of organizations he studied, including unexpected jobs like computer programming. Further analysis showed that emotional competencies were twice as important contributors to excellence than pure intellect and expertise. Goleman found that emotional intelligence is even more important for leadership. He says that emotional intelligence separates mediocre leaders from the best leaders, and his analysis showed that close to 90 percent of the success of star performers could be attributed to emotional intelligence.

Goleman defines an emotional competence as "a learned capability based on emotional intelligence that results in outstanding performance at work" (1998: 24). Goleman describes five dimensions of emotional intelligence, which include a total of twenty-five emotional competencies. The dimensions and their associated competencies are:

Self-Awareness: Knowing one's internal states, preferences, resources, and intuitions. Associated emotional competencies: emotional awareness, accurate self-assessment, and self-confidence.

Self-Regulation: Managing one's internal states, impulses, and resources. Associated emotional competencies: self-control, trustworthiness, conscientiousness, adaptability, and innovation.

Motivation: Emotional tendencies that guide or facilitate reaching goals. Associated emotional competencies: achievement drive, commitment, initiative, optimism.

Empathy: Awareness of others' feelings, needs, and concerns. Associated emotional competencies: understanding others, developing others, service orientation, leveraging diversity, political awareness.

Social Skills: Adeptness at inducing desirable responses in others. Associated emotional competencies: influence, communication, conflict management, leadership, change catalyst, building bonds, collaboration and cooperation, and team capabilities. (Adapted from Goleman 1998: 26–27)

It seems natural for people pursuing passion to seek insight into their own capacity for healthy emotions. There are 360-degree inventories measuring emotional intelligence available that can provide feedback about your own emotional competence.

Genuineness.   Chapter 5 discussed the role of genuineness. Everyone wears masks to a degree, plays roles, and puts on a show for peers, supervisors, and even family members. True passion flows from genuineness. Ask yourself if you are moving toward or away from being genuine. Will the activities you are planning to achieve your passion move you toward your natural self, or further away? Test your plans against trends that Carl Rogers found in his clients.

1. *Moving Away from Facades.* Are you hiding less of your real self as you move toward passionate work? Or more?
2. *Moving Away from "Oughts."* Are you doing more of what your parents, supervisor, spouse, or friends think you "ought" to be doing? Are you what people think you "ought to be"? Or are you moving toward what you really are and what you really want to do?
3. *Moving Away from Meeting Expectations.* People are constantly norming themselves, moving themselves toward the societal average because of cultural norms, values, and standards. Are you moving toward meeting your own expectations and being your own unique, special self?
4. *Moving Away from Pleasing Others.* "I find that many individuals have formed themselves by trying to please others . . . " (Rogers 1961: 170). Are you designing your life increasingly around pleasing your own true self, and not what others expect?
5. *Moving Toward Self-Direction.* Are you becoming more autonomous, more responsible for yourself, more toward making your own choices and accepting the consequences?
6. *Moving Toward Being Process.* "Clients seem to move toward more openly being a process, a fluidity, a changing. They are not disturbed to find that they are not the same from day to day. . . . They are in flux, and seem more content to continue in

this flowing current. The striving for conclusions and end states seems to diminish" (171). Are you a work in progress? Are you designing your life to be evolutionary and sometimes even revolutionary?

7. *Moving Toward Being Complexity.* Are you examining your assumptions and looking for multiple perspectives? Are you cognizant of the richness of the moment?

8. *Moving Toward Openness to Experience.* Are you afraid of experience and of experiencing or are you becoming increasingly open to new feelings, different perspectives, awareness of the situation, and appreciative of all that life and work have to offer?

9. *Moving Toward Acceptance of Others.* Being open to yourself is one side, but how open are you to the experiences of others, how accepting of their views, nonjudgmental about the fullness of their lives?

10. *Moving Toward Trust of Self.* Are you becoming increasingly trusting and valuing of the process that is yourself? "Time and again in my clients, I have seen simple people become significant and creative in their own spheres, as they have developed more trust of the processes going on within themselves, and have dared to feel their own feelings, live by values which they discover within, and express themselves in their own unique ways."

(Adapted from Rogers 1961: 167–175)

Not being genuine takes its toll. Putting on a facade, a "work face" every day, requires emotional effort. It is work to maintain a public persona that does not reflect true feelings. It requires energy to act chipper or friendly on the job when one feels angry or depressed inside. Hochschild defines this as emotional labor. Emotional labor is ". . . the management of feeling to create a publicly observable facial and bodily display . . . " (1983: 7). Emotional labor—smiles and sunny attitudes in the cases of people like flight attendants or customer service representatives, or aggressiveness on the part of a bill collector—has, according to Hochschild, exchange value. It is worth something. Employers hire people who can display these char-acteristics because it helps the organization to achieve its goals.

But emotional labor can carry a price. It means managing emotions—either inducing or suppressing feelings—in order to give the client-boss-customer-coworker-debtor or whomever, the emotional display deemed appropriate for the situation. At some point, the individual may ask herself what is real—the person acting out emotions that are not genuinely felt or the person inside. Emotional labor can result in emotional numbness and burnout. It may result in withdrawal. The person may refuse to act out at all (with subsequent career implications).

Every job calls for some emotional labor, even if the main task isn't to work with customers. Useful interactions with coworkers require a civility that might be artificially produced from time to time. Who hasn't felt ill or had a personal problem that had to be submerged in order to get along with coworkers? Sometimes it takes too much effort. We simply rely upon the goodwill of others and lapse into grumpiness or a moodiness that wouldn't be tolerated if those modes were our standard. Even with our closest friends and relatives we put on masks. No one wants to be around someone who constantly wears his emotions on his sleeve.

Emotionally intelligent people have the ability to be both genuine and also socially competent. With our closest confidants we are allowed to express grief, fear, hope, love, and desire. Expressing these emotions is usually not tolerated in the workplace. The mere expression of emotion is often frowned upon. In that climate passion is verboten, individual excitement is normed out of accepted behavior, and people follow social cues rather than spontaneously responding. Emotions are often sanitized.

Are you serious about assessing your own genuineness? Ask others whether they perceive you as a genuine or a superficial person. Do they think you are trustworthy? Do they think you are being you at work? Can they get behind the mask? Most people will have an opinion about how genuine you really are.

Exterior Design

Assessing Your Opportunities.   Having a good handle on your own skills, knowledge, character, and willpower is a prerequisite for success. You will also need to understand the job market, how to be successful in a particular profession or craft, what the barriers to entry are, and what will be happening in your chosen field a few years from now.

You have identified the passionate work you wish to pursue. Now find out everything you can about it. What does it pay? What is the competition for available jobs? Who hires people for those jobs? Where are most of the jobs located geographically? Are you willing to move there? What are the prospects for moving into other interesting work over time? Will the work become obsolete? With what kind of people would you work side by side every day? What are the other rewards or disincentives you might expect over time?

Do a thorough analysis, think about it, talk to people who do it and have done it, and decide what the best courses of action might be to achieve it.

Planning.   Once you've thoroughly looked at yourself (interior work) and thoroughly looked at your potential careers, employment trends, and family situation (external work), you can begin to design how you will build a life of passionate work. What will your strategy to accomplish your dream career be?

For an organization, strategy "is the pattern of organizational moves and managerial approaches used to achieve organizational objectives and to pursue the organization's mission" (Thompson and Strickland 1992: 7). For an individual designing a life, strategy is everything you map out to attain and sustain passionate work. Those plans may be very different for different people. They may include going to school to learn new skills and knowledge, finding a mentor to help you learn the ins and outs of what you wish to do, unearthing a career counselor to help you understand your strengths and weaknesses and to develop a career plan, or taking on new assignments within your organization. There may be a number of routes that lead to your final destination. You must choose the path that makes the most sense for you. The path is likely to change along the way. The more you have prepared, the more likely it is that you will find alternate detours that work.

What will your strategy be? What happens if what you thought would be fun turns out to be merely stressful? Can you test the waters, perhaps by volunteering or by observing or interviewing someone who is currently doing what you aspire to do? Informational interviews can give you powerful insight into what you are proposing to yourself. How can you best learn about the opportunities and the pitfalls?

Strategy may include thinking about what you want to accomplish by when. What's your game plan? Who do you need to get to know? By hanging around people who are already doing what you want to do, you will learn from them both directly and vicariously. What resources will you need? Student loans, small business loans, a year's worth of savings, a network of potential contacts, or something as simple as a vehicle or a personal computer? What credentials will you need?

Developing Alternatives.   What is your strategy for achieving the passionate work you have envisioned? Seldom does the original plan remain unchanged. If you know from the start that things won't go as planned then it will be less daunting when obstacles occur that force you to change. There are at least three basic strategic routes to achieving passionate work, with a number of variations between them.

Make Your Current Job or Task More Passionate.   For a variety of good reasons, you may decide to stay in your current position, at least for a while. It may be that you've already found the work that you love. That would be wonderful. It may be that you are working in this position in order to prepare for a future that you've imagined (see underwriting, below). It may be that you thought that your work was deadly, but that upon reflection, you see that it has possibilities or that you are simply in a slump. It may be that the financial penalties are so severe that you choose not to leave. It may be that you just have to put bread on the table right now. For whatever reason, you choose to remain where you are. Staying where you are can be very exciting. One dental hygienist told us that "What made a change for me was realizing that I can make a difference—together or alone. . . . Once I found that I can encourage and support myself and seek out those with the same motivation, I had a much more positive outlook." Another person took advantage of a potentially debilitating situation. "I was employed by a program that, in my opinion, was underdeveloped. It was a federally funded grant program. As my supervisor's performance declined with personal issues, I stepped in, directed the program, and made some very positive and effective changes. I was very passionate about my work at this time."

Some jobs are inherently more repetitious and require more oversight than others. Some jobs have more variety, more freedom than others. Virtually any circumstance, however, can be used to increase passion for the task. The processes we've discussed in this book—look for learning opportunities, sources of meaning, joy—can be applied to most situations.

Rhonda Neel has created a workshop called "Take Your Job from Ordinary to Extraordinary" for call center employees. She says that one way to increase job satisfaction is to turn the job into a more complex activity. "People who play with and transform the opportunities in their surroundings," she says, "have much more enjoyable experiences than those who feel they can't alter their realities." Neel also asks employees to transform their jobs by making a game of it. "The more work resembles a game," she says, "the more enjoyable it will be." In workshops, she asks them to develop two games that they can play at work.

Even in the direst situations, the work or the situation itself can be made more meaningful, more challenging, relationships more significant, the day more fun, and activities more creative. A pediatric coordinator told us, "I like discovering new and effective ways of providing quality education and pleasant experience."

Quit What You Are Doing and Begin Something New. This is the approach with the most immediate risk. It could be argued that sitting in a passionless situation for too long has far greater risk than this alternative, but simply leaving what you are doing now has financial risks and personal risks, could adversely affect your family both in the short and long term, and it could turn out to be a decision that just doesn't lead to passionate work. If you choose this approach, which may be the perfect choice for you, it is best to do it with eyes wide open. Although there are many stories of successful people leaping off of vocational cliffs and landing safely, many people have also crashed and burned.

If you choose this path, ask yourself how you can hedge your risk. A husband and wife we talked to were both unhappy in their jobs. They decided that the husband would quit work immediately and that the wife would be the source of their security until he established his new career, which was to work with racing cars. Soon he had worked his way into a successful position and she quit her job to start a successful consulting company. Now, they told us, both of them are immeasurably happy with their work, they travel around the country, meet interesting people, and have challenging jobs. Another person in her twenties found passion by "founding and developing my nonprofit organization." Quitting your current job, given the right circumstances, can give you immense sources for passionate work. A fifty-four-year-old medical coding analyst "transferred to another department where my job was to identify improper billing and report it. I felt once again a renewed passion for the task and a sense of empowerment that I may be able to effect a change for the better."

Not everyone has the luxury of a husband-wife team that can support each other while each finds his or her passion, but most people have options. If you quit your job today, do you already have something lined up? Do you have savings that you can draw on until you are on your feet? Do you have a contingency plan? What will you do if your original plan doesn't work out? You ultimately want to do work that you can be passionate about doing. Do your contingency plans still lead you in that direction? Be clear in your mind what you are prepared to sacrifice and for what you need to make arrangements. Are you willing to lose a marriage, your family, or your social life to achieve your dreams? Many people have, and regretted it later. Others have been willing to pay that price and felt themselves amply rewarded. If you are willing to go that far, it makes the long hours, perhaps time away from home, and less immediate and enduring income easier to handle if that is what is required. If you aren't willing to sacrifice these personal relationships, how will you mitigate the impact? Will the quality of your lives be higher so that you are willing to sacrifice income?

Underwrite Your Future Job with Your Current Job. Sometimes it just doesn't make sense to simply give two weeks' notice, and yet it's an emotional death sentence to give up and stay where you are. Underwriting the next job or other passionate work with your current job is another important strategy. Underwriting your next job means using your current job to gain the information, develop the resources, and meet the people that will be required to move on successfully. It does *not* mean doing anything unethical (like taking proprietary information or key accounts). It simply means using the situation you are in to prepare yourself for the future. This, of course, is what should occur in all three scenarios. Here it is the priority.

Smart people make their current employers successful while at the same time preparing for the future. People who have few options perceive themselves to be helpless. By developing many options and employability, you become more valuable to your current employer and more marketable at the same time. Ways of preparing include taking company-sponsored training programs, cross-training with other jobs, or taking on new or additional responsibilities that will increase your marketability.

If you give yourself enough time, you can accomplish seeming miracles. If you were asked to play a professional-level piano concerto at Carnegie Hall next month, you would probably fail. But if you were asked to do it ten years from now for a reward of a million dollars, you would likely find ways to accomplish it. You would literally make thousands and thousands of decisions that would further your ability to achieve the goal, because the reward was significant and you had the time. Time gives you personal power. If you are underwriting your next career, begin now. It may take six months, a year, or even ten years, but you probably have a much higher chance of succeeding if you stay the course than you might believe (see Figure 6.1).

FIGURE 6.1   Time/Control Relationship

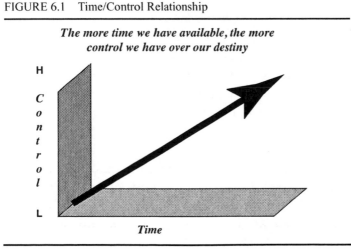

We heard an interesting story about the Designing process while making a "Passionate Work" presentation one evening. We asked the group if anyone had designed a passionate career. One woman waved her hand. "I always wanted to own a bed-and-breakfast," she said, "but I had no idea how to do it." She went on, describing to the audience all of the activities she undertook to achieve her dream. They involved such things as learning about financing, working in the bed-and-breakfast business, and learning from people experienced in the industry. "Now," she concluded, "ten years later I own my own bed-and-breakfast."

Designing for Organizations

Are your employees on autopilot? Are they just getting through the day? Have you helped them to truly understand the talents and abilities that they bring to the workplace? Do they feel powerful or powerless? Why? Are you contributing to either feeling? What can you do as an organizational leader or human resource development professional to design your own passionate work environment?

Passionate Work Environments

Occupational Intimacy requires meaningful work, work that you love, and a nurturing environment. Successful organizations intentionally create environments that facilitate, sometimes even mandate, passionate work. Collins and Porras studied visionary companies and found that they display four characteristics of cults more than other comparison companies do. Visionary companies typically have (1) a fervently held ideology, (2) an indoctrination process into the core ideology, (3) tightness of fit—rewards for those who fit and negative reinforcements for those who do not, and (4) elitism—a sense of being part of something special for those inside the organization. These organizations, Collins and Porras emphasize, are not cults, but have some cultlike attributes.

They give as examples IBM, which, by the 1930s had "fully institutionalized its indoctrination process and created a full-fledged 'schoolhouse' that is used to socialize and train future officers of the company" (1997: 124); Disney, which, among other processes, thoroughly screens and socializes hourly theme park workers; requires every single employee to attend a new employee orientation called Disney Traditions; has its own special language (employees are "cast members," for example); and reinforces elitism by shrouding "its inner workings in secrecy" (130). "Indeed, when examining Disney, it can be hard to keep in mind that it is a corporation, not a social or religious movement" (130); and Proctor and Gamble, which has both formal and informal indoctrination processes, requires all employees to read its official biography, immediately socializes new hires by having them work closely with other members of the company "the company's relatively isolated location in a P&G-dominated city (Cincinnati) further reinforces the sense of complete immersion into the company" (132), has "paternalistic and progressive pay and benefit programs which bind its people closely to the company" (130), and has an "intense penchant" for secrecy and control of information" (134). Porras and Collins conclude that the goal is to "build an organization that fervently preserves its core ideology in specific, concrete ways" (135), by using tangible mechanisms that reinforce it.

Each passionate environment is different and meets differing needs of differing people. Strong, powerful, passionate environments eject like a virus people who don't fit (Collins and Porras 1997). The risk and opportunity for individuals here is that people who are clear about what makes them passionate can clearly and quickly identify whether they will fit in and either join or leave on their own terms. People, however, who are not clear run the risk of being subsumed by the corporation. Those people will either lead marginal employment existences by trying to fit in when they don't or will at some point be asked to leave.

Organizations that do not have a strong, clear, passionate environment, on the other hand, do not send clear signals to employees and potential employees. It is more difficult to know if there is a fit or not. Passionate work is not nurtured. If it exists it is coincidental. Employees don't have anything to anchor their potential for passion to and many times drift along, sometimes for years, before recognizing that their careers have been marginal, trivialized, or wasted. Passionate organizations are not ambivalent, not unclear, and not wishy-washy. They take a stand about what they stand for and build the organization around that stance. By making choices and being founded on passion, organizations provide the ecology for passionate employees to thrive.

What are some of the elements involved in designing a passionate work environment? The next section will review organizational pitfalls—areas that if not attended to can suck the passion out of employees; rewards; and organizational learning.

Pitfalls Revisited

Our research found four pitfalls to passionate work. In every case the opposite response will foster passionate work. This is true both for individual planning and for organizational support.

Freedom Rather Than Overcontrol. Empowerment is a continuum. The more external control, the less empowerment. The more freedom, the more empowerment. Empowering environments cultivate passion. The key to empowerment is to increasingly give employees responsibility and authority for their work dependant on their abilities and character. The Situational Leadership Model (Blanchard, Zigarmi, and Zigarmi 1994) and Stephen Covey's (1989) Win-Win Agreements are two frameworks for supporting this development. The situational leadership model demonstrates how supervisors can move, or individuals can move themselves, from being primarily directed as an enthusiastic beginner to being primarily delegated to as a peak performer. Win-Win Agreements are Covey's mechanism for providing increasing levels of empowerment by providing fewer and fewer guidelines and controls for the individual through clear direction, guidelines, and desired outcomes; understanding available resources; accountability; and consequences. To the extent that organizations impose obstacles to empowerment, passion will be reduced proportionally. A forty-nine-year-old woman told us that as a program director her passion was unleashed when "I was given room to create new programs and strengthen present ones." No matter what the nature of your organization is, work toward progressively freeing your employees. Allow them to find creative ways to solve problems or meet goals.

Meaningful Work Rather Than Meaningless/Boring Work. Meaningful work has been discussed at length above because meaningfulness, along with a nurturing environment and joyous work, are the three legs of occupational intimacy. Think, though, a bit more broadly about what makes any activity consequential. Religious groups, political parties, advocacy groups, athletic teams, and marketers all have found ways to make otherwise mundane goals, tasks, or activities into something heavy with meaning. They build significance through ritual, special events, icons, and metaphor. Symbolism makes otherwise trite activities rich; just-another-day into Mother's Day; a clanging bell or a burning candle into a link to a higher power; a Celtic cross, a dove, or beads as representative of something powerful; uniforms, insignias, bracelets, tattoos, hairstyles, use of colors, music, or slogans as common bonds that tie teams, communities, countries, armies, or organizations together. Rituals are powerful vehicles to make events, people, and processes significant. Ritualistic prayers or team cheers before a game, religious ceremonies, initiation rites for new organizational members, family traditions, and organizational team-building activities all intensify meaning, membership, and sense of purpose.

Part of developing meaningful work concerns finding an exciting vision and mission for employees that is inspiring. Even the most mundane work can be meaningful if it is done in the context of an exciting end result. When Southwest Airlines was first formed, perhaps this vision was the primary source of meaning for employees.

> These people *believed.* They took a risk and joined a company that had no track record. They bet their careers when the stakes were high; they gave their time when getting a paycheck wasn't guaranteed; they gambled their reputations when the media were doubtful. They were nutty, flashy, and very hip when the competition was conventional, businesslike, and very bland. These originals set the pace and the pattern of Southwest's way of doing business. They believed that if they just worked hard enough, that if Southwest Airlines were just different enough, that if they just cared enough, the company would pull through. Joy Bardo, senior administrative coordinator, believes that it was just a matter of love: "It was a dream that started for all of us. We were focused on trying to do the best job we could because we wanted to see the dream come alive." (Freiberg and Freiberg 1996: 37)

How does your organization build meaning into otherwise routine activities? How does your organization recognize the significance of events? Passionate organizations find or develop symbols, rituals, metaphors, or slogans to which people can anchor their emotions. Learning is also a part of what makes work interesting and meaningful instead of boring.

Boring work is generally repetitious, exhausting, can be depressing, and if at times it doesn't foster mindlessness, it can foster anger—sometimes going so far as what has become known as "going postal." Boredom occurs when the learning curve has slowed to a virtual standstill. Boredom is a function of having too little to learn. Increased learning reduces boredom and increases passion. Reduced learning increases boredom and decreases passion. Ideally, learning will be work related but, even if it isn't, it will increase "secondhand" passion. Sometimes, simply playing inner mind games (like challenging yourself to complete a task faster or more creatively each time) will increase an employee's learning and therefore increased interest in the work.

Rhonda Neel gives an example of such a game for a customer service representative. "Listen to the tone of the caller. Rate the tone as 1 being very calm to 10 being very angry. Keep monitoring the caller throughout the call and see if the tone changes in response to your professionalism. The goal of the call will be to see if you can calm down an upset caller and by how much."

Fabricating work games can be effective too. "Take Your Job from Ordinary to Extraordinary," the workshop Neel developed for call center employees, uses games to make the work more enjoyable, just as Southwest Airlines is famous for using songs, games, and other entertainment to interest both employees and passengers.

Other organizations find ways to learn from every situation, perhaps by reviewing the day or the project and doing a postmortem to find out what can be learned from the situation and improved upon. Perhaps they facilitate workforce learning by engaging employees in anticipating future situations and studying how to approach them differently, or by investigating ways to improve interpersonal relationships. Prisoners in concentration camps, bereft of opportunities to learn, may manufacture ways to do it, from visualizing a golf game to developing secret means of communication.

Problems produce opportunities for learning. When people give up on the problem or are laissez-faire, then ennui is the story of the day, the period in a life or even a lifetime. Any situation, however restrictive, can provide opportunities for learning. True, some environments are far richer fields for learning. Organizational leaders should be working toward these. If necessary, however, employers should consider creating learning opportunities that might not be directly related to the job or the organization. Otherwise, the narcotic of boredom becomes too addictive and your employees will find themselves years later feeling like their lives were wasted. In the short run, they are likely to sit on their hands, just waiting for instructions, when you want them to take charge.

From an organizational perspective, employees who are bored to tears will be less productive than those who are not. How will you draw new employees into a deadly dull organization? It can be a deadly spiral—lack of learning leads to boredom, which lowers motivation to learn, then to acceptance of the situation, which then leads to further lack of learning and further boredom. For an individual, the end result might ultimately be a good one even if undesirable for many other reasons—he gets fired because everyone else is so much further ahead, and then is forced to learn in order to be employable. As an employer, however, you have to recruit, hire, and train a new employee.

Continuous learning and work environments that are supportive of learning are important for Generation X employees (Bova and Kroth 1999) and the generations coming up behind them. Generation X employees want work to be constantly challenging and continually cause them to stretch. Generation X employees prefer action learning. That is, they would rather learn by doing and working to solve real workplace problems (Bova and Kroth 2001) instead of sitting in a classroom. GenXers' second learning preference is incidental learning, which is usually a by-product of something else, often working situations, and their third choice is formal or traditional learning. Bova and Kroth identify enablers for Generation X learning in each of the modes: For action learning, enablers are reflection, real problems, and group learning. For incidental learning they are reflection, open-mindedness, and a culture of forgiveness and risk-taking. For formal learning enablers are having materials geared to Generation X preferences, self-directed learning (e-learning, for example), and learning activities that are fun, challenging, and flexible. Surrounding each of these learning modes and enablers, Bova and Kroth say, are factors that "lubricate" (2001: 63) the learning

FIGURE 6.2   The Generation X Learning Model—Gearing Up for Generation X

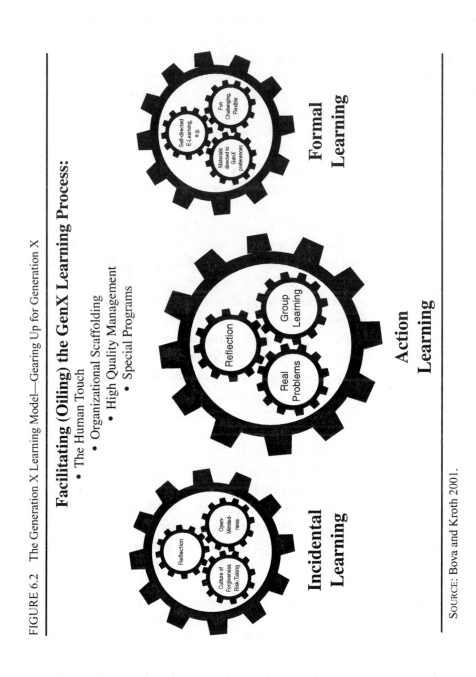

Facilitating (Oiling) the GenX Learning Process:
- The Human Touch
  - Organizational Scaffolding
  - High Quality Management
  - Special Programs

Incidental Learning

Action Learning

Formal Learning

processes for Generation X employees. Those factors are the human touch, organizational scaffolding, high quality management, and special programs. These factors facilitate learning, ease transitions, and maximize each of the learning modes both singularly and interrelatedly. Bova and Kroth developed a model to capture how these concepts relate to each other. This model depicts the learning preferences, enablers, and surrounding factors for Generation X that were described above (see Figure 6.2).

Perhaps most important, learning is what humanizes us and makes work not only interesting and important but is an important link to who we are as human beings. Providing a learning environment for your employees touches the very soul of the organization. Apps says:

> Many of us have never realized that learning can make us human, can help us get up each day with anticipation and excitement, and can help us live our days with meaning rather than with remorse, guilt, and a host of other demons that drag us down and make us less than we can be." (1996: 26)

One of the most powerful ways that organizations can support individual learning is through assessments. Companies can offer assessment through comprehensive career centers, personal coaching, annual personal development planning, or on an ad hoc basis for key internal talent. By helping employees identify learning gaps and then providing the means to fill them, organizations build organizational capacity and increase the individual's interest in the job and the organization.

Learning is the essence of passionate work.

Scaffolding Support Rather Than Fostering Inadequacy. Every person has basic feelings of adequacy or inadequacy depending on the situation and also has a general feeling about her or his own abilities. Organizations either reduce feelings of inadequacy via their actions or they increase it. Much depends on being sensitive to the needs of the particular individual in a particular situation. It is difficult for a person to feel passionately about something she or he feels incompetent about doing.

Bova and Kroth, speaking of Generation X employees, say that "The trick is to provide the employee just the right scaffolding—the support he or she needs and not too much or too little—for every situation. Too much support breeds dependence, or the micromanagement a Generation Xer abhors. Too little support is risky for employee and organization alike—while we learn from failure, some failures are unnecessary and cause long-lasting scars" (2001: 64).

Companies promote scaffolding when they formalize mentoring programs, provide just-in-time or other practical training, develop communities of learning, or facilitate support groups. One of the most powerful vehicles for employee scaffolding is comprehensive employee developmental planning. Developmental planning that involves several senior managers assessing the skills, talents, and characteristics of an employee, and then creating a long-term plan to give that person experiences that will stretch but not snap the individual, creates organizational commitment to that employee. When thinking about the developmental progress of employees, it is helpful to consider the employee not just a member of a department or function but also a member of the organizational community. As a member of the community, formal and informal leaders take it upon themselves to advise, challenge, support, shake up, collaborate with, and share wisdom with the employee. As a member of the larger community, the employee escapes being considered the property of a particular department, function, or leader, but is, rather, accessible to the entire organization for assignments, networking, and other developmental processes.

Trusting Environment Rather Than Manipulation, Dishonesty, Lack of Trust.   Trust is the emotional glue that allows people to interact most effectively with each other. It underpins all long-term, successful relationships. It allows the creativity, wisdom, and energy of individuals to emerge from hiding, and latent group synergy to evolve into something powerful.

Organizations are made up of people. Therefore relationships, both long-term and virtual, are key to organizational success. Employees will not bring their whole selves to work unless they feel safe. We all wear masks that constrain communication, for very good reasons. They protect us; they tell others what hat we are wearing. But when masks inhibit the free flow of information and communication is stilted, they are counterproductive. When work environments are poisonous, the masks are on everywhere as people protect themselves from harm.

Building trusting environments, where people feel safe to express themselves and to be themselves as much as possible, is essential to passionate work. Passionate work, by definition, requires making oneself vulnerable to success or failure, to expressing joy or pain, and to being genuine. Dishonest, manipulative environments discourage those behaviors.

Lack of trust is insidious. In this situation, people have a hard time figuring out how to create trust. Everyone blames each other and often no one is willing to take responsibility for beginning the healing process. Who is responsible in an organization to develop a trusting environment? The most practical answer is that you are responsible, whoever you are and whatever your position. Naturally, the potential to cultivate or destroy trust increases the higher in the organization one looks, but the power resides in every individual.

The first step is to recognize that trust in a relationship begins by being trustworthy. Exercise integrity—do what you say that you will do, time and again—and you will build trust in your own relationships. Your word will be your bond. Be as open as you can be about your intentions and avoid manipulation like the plague. Your policies and procedures, your strategies and tactics, your rewards and recognition should be as transparent as possible, and rigorously adhered to in order to assure that employees believe in them. Leaders, following these simple precepts, can have enormous influence. People don't have to agree with an action or a direction or a policy, but if they can count on them to be conducted with integrity, then they can trust the people, the practices, and the system itself.

Rewards and Recognition

Sternberg says that "Probably the strongest learning mechanism for the buildup of passionate response is the mechanism of intermittent reinforcement" (1987: 44–45). Intermittent reinforcement, he says, is even more powerful than continuous reinforcement. When we talk with groups of people about what fosters passion, rewards and recognition are inevitably mentioned. Ask a group of unpaid community actors why they spend hours and hours after work to be in shows, and one of the main reasons they give is the applause.

Every person is different. For some, the intrinsic reward of doing work that is joyful, meaningful, and genuine is the ultimate prize that sustains passion over time. For others, extrinsic rewards such as recognition—a plaque or medal for an employee or an athlete, applause for an actor (or an Oscar, or a magazine cover, or an appearance on *Letterman,* for example)—are the sources of passion over time. One otherwise confident, assertive employee broke down and cried when she didn't receive the monetary reward she thought she deserved. She told us that it had nothing to do with the money itself, but that she felt the organization didn't value her or her contributions. Money was her yardstick. It told her whether she was important. Organizations must intentionally incorporate a variety of rewards and recognition into the workplace to meet the variety of individual needs.

Organizations can provide powerful conditions for motivating employees, creating the appropriate expectations by being clear about expected rewards and then by actually fulfilling those expectations. Individuals, of course, often forget the easiest approach—to reward themselves for their successes.

Developing Alternatives for Employees—Organizational View

Your employees are thinking about how they can work toward jobs that offer passionate work. That means valuable talent may leave your company that will be difficult to replace. How can you respond effectively to the alternatives discussed above?

Make Your Current Job or Task More Passionate—Organizational View. As an organization, this is the alternative you would prefer your employees to pursue. Provide as much support and creative ways for employees to make their current jobs more enjoyable. Some things the individual cannot provide. Some things only the organization can do.

Organizations can be creative about job responsibilities—look for ways to provide variety in the work, link employees with customers so that they can see results, cross-train employees, provide lots of recognition and rewards, find sources of fun and play, make the mission and vision of the organization inspiring and the goals challenging. A twenty-five-year-old restaurant manager has the right idea. "I can't compete with others for money, but I can bring energy, excitement, and a sincere feeling of care and courage to my employees." That's the way to help reinvigorate passion for employees in their current jobs.

Quit What You Are Doing and Begin Something New—Organizational View. Many organizations can reduce the risk of employees leaving their jobs by encouraging them to change jobs within the organization and providing opportunities to do it. Paul Shirley, who eventually became one of the founders of a successful high-tech company, began his career in the air force. After reenlisting, they shipped him to Denver to become a teacher of electronics. They eventually sent him back to Purdue to get his degree in electrical engineering and then he came to work in Albuquerque at the air force's Airborne Laser Laboratory. "Here I am," he said, "in a very structured environment called the U.S. Air Force, but yet I walk into an assignment that is full of research and development . . . though I was the new kid on the block, second lieutenant, I was offered the opportunity to do whatever I really wanted to do." He eventually went back to get his master's degree and when he finished that, he was assigned to teach electrical engineering at the Air Force Academy. Soon he got a call to work in Washington at the Strategic Defense Initiative, eventually becoming program manager. Throughout his career he received different and interesting assignments.

Especially early in a career, organizations can help employees test new jobs, take on new tasks, go to different courses, or provide mentors or coaching in new situations, so that trying new responsibilities becomes normal rather than the exception. The larger the employee's knowledge base, and therefore the more valuable the employee to the organization, the more willing she or he will be to change jobs if the organization thinks there might be a fit between company and employee needs.

Underwrite Your Future Job with Your Current Job—Organizational View. Your employee is using everything at his disposal in his current job to get ready for the next job, which may or may not be inside your company. Is your response to restrict him? To cut him off from information? To not allow him to talk to others in or outside the company? Unless we are talking about highly competitive, strategic information or connections, the answer is no.

First of all, you can't be sure which of your employees are looking for the next job and which are just aggressive on the job. If you restrain learning and networking, it will be chilling for everyone. You stop productivity in its tracks.

Second, if you do happen to know that someone is trying to build a résumé or organizational successes or contacts in order to move to the job . . . rejoice. That person is likely to be more productive. She is learning more, trying to apply what she's learning, and needs accomplishments. One of the vocations of a leader, and the responsibility of every manager, is to develop people. Good leaders see people they have developed leaving for greener pastures all the time. Of course, the best and the brightest know who they want to work for too—the person who encourages their growth and career success. Great leaders draw the best talent to them.

Last, even if your employee leaves, he may be a future resource for you. He will appreciate your support and will be more likely to support you if you need him for future work, advice, or contacts. Always encourage the person who is trying to move to a position where he or she can thrive. Otherwise, you will always be stuck with people who don't really want to be there.

Organizational Learning

The qualities of a learning organization provide a framework for looking at designing passionate work environments. Consider how important learning is to passionate work. The organization that systematically encourages learning is more likely to have a passionate organization.

Gilley and Maycunich (2000) say that a learning organization is an institution that "learns powerfully and collectively, continually transforming itself to better manage and use knowledge for corporate success, empowering people within and outside the organization to learn as they work and to utilize technology to maximize learning and production" (14). They go on, however, to describe what they believe to be the next evolutionary step beyond a learning organization—the developmental organization. The developmental organization "really means to foster an environment in which employee growth and development is paramount, that is, to create conditions in which employees are encouraged, rewarded, and appreciated for their individual growth and development" (22). Leaders in developmental organizations have a philosophy that supports lifelong commitment to employees and their well-being.

What are the qualities of a learning organization and how do they relate to passionate work environments? We can draw on the characteristics of what are being described as learning organizations to learn more about what makes an environment that nurtures employees.

According to Watkins and Marsick (1993), learning organizations must:

- Create continuous learning opportunities
- Promote inquiry and dialogue
- Encourage collaboration and team learning
- Establish systems to capture and share learning
- Empower people toward a collective vision
- Connect the organization to its environment
  (1993: 11)

Passionate people are continuously learning, are constantly stretching, and trying new things. Learning organizations foster these qualities. New work assignments, job rotations, project opportunities, and innovative thinking are embedded consciously or unconsciously in learning organizations. Dialogue and inquiry—asking questions that explore more than probe—are honored in organizations that believe that success depends on understanding, multiple perspectives, and challenging the status quo. Accepting little or nothing as inalienable, learning organizations at the same time continually build depth of wisdom and knowledge. Working in such surroundings is energizing, challenging, and often inspiring. A focus on continuous learning signifies an organization's intent to develop its employees, and therefore means that employees are important.

EXERCISE TWELVE: Designing—Individual

Creating the Blueprint

Living your life's work is analogous to designing a house. First you visualize it (Discovering), then you have to draw up the plans for it (Designing), and finally you have to build it (Developing). Hopefully, by now you have an idea of what your passionate work could be. The purpose of these exercises is to help you start to draw up the plans.

Rate your readiness to create your blueprint for passionate work from 1 (not ready) to 5 (fully ready).

Assessing

_____I am ready to take full responsibility for my life, to stop blaming others for my situation, and to take the consequences, good or bad, for my decisions.

_____I understand that transitioning to a new life's work requires "stick-to-itive-ness," and I have developed the willpower and determination to fulfill my plans.

_____I have studied and have a deep understanding of the requirements for my desired, passionate work. I have studied and have a deep understanding of the job market for the kind of work I am pursuing.

_____I have critically looked at my current skills, knowledge, abilities, relationships, and financial situation in relationship to the ones required to achieve my desired work. I know well what the gaps are between where I am and where I need to be.

Planning

_____I have developed a plan (preferably written) for how I will bridge the gaps I uncovered. I have an excellent understanding of the alternatives that are possible, contingency plans, and the risks involved.

_____If I choose to remain in my current job, I have talked extensively with people, studied the potential for the kind of work I do, and developed a plan for how I will make my current job more passionate.

_____If I choose to leave my current job and start something new, I have talked extensively with people, studied the potential for the kind of work I do, prepared myself financially, gained support from significant others, assessed the risks, and developed a plan for how I will transition from one job or company to another.

_____If I choose to underwrite a future job with my current job, I have looked at all the ways that I can mutually benefit my current organization and myself while I prepare for my desired next job.

____Regardless of the path I've chosen, my plan includes specific goals and objectives with a timetable, a strategy to get there, an understanding of the risks and how to mitigate them, and an assessment of the gaps I have to overcome.

EXERCISE THIRTEEN: Designing—Organizations

Creating the Blueprint
Organizations have the challenge of creating passionate work environments—places where employees experience Occupational Intimacy. The purpose of this exercise is to help you start to create those surroundings.

Describe what your organization would look and feel like if it were a passionate work environment. What would employees be doing? Leaders? What would your building look like? What kind of policies, procedures, and guidelines would be in place? What kind of celebrations would occur? How would your supervisors manage? What kind of tools and equipment would your employees have access to? What would the spirit of the place be like? Describe it in detail.

Assessment
Now that you have described your desired passionate situation, list the ten most important things that would have to happen for it to become reality. (Think of policies, programs, management/leadership, incentives, and so on.)

1.
2.
3.
4.
5.
6.
7.
8.
9.
10.

Now go back and highlight the three that, if accomplished, would make the biggest difference in your organization.

Now go back and circle the three that you have the most ability to influence.

Now go back and put a checkmark next to the three that are the easiest to accomplish.

Analyze your work. Are there any items that are highlighted, circled, *and* checked? Mark them as "winners!"

Analyze some more and write down your best strategy for making your organization one that reinforces passion for work.

My strategy for creating (or reinforcing) a passionate work environment in our organization is:

The Developing Process

By annihilating the desires, you annihilate the mind. Every man without passions has within him no principle of action, nor motive to act.

—CLAUDE ADRIEN, *Helvetius*

Once we have discovered where our passions lie and have designed a process or plan for living them, it is time to take the giant step of actually putting that plan into action. The last three Keys—Risking, Learning, and Building Self-Efficacy—are the series of activities that help us to take that step and continue to live a life of passion. Together they comprise our third major process—Developing. This Developing process is indispensable to maintaining our passion and to reigniting it when it starts to flag. Some people go through these steps almost unconsciously—they are the people we admire because they always seem to be living their life fully. A forty-four-year-old astronomer we interviewed said that when his passion is waning, "Then I have to find something unique, difficult, and long-term in order to rekindle it and not be going through the motions." Most of us, however, have to learn how to help ourselves and to develop the skills we need to live life more fully.

These three processes cannot be separated from each other. As we risk, we learn; as we learn, we gain more confidence; as we gain more confidence, we take larger risks. We sometimes learn that we need to take more risks, and sometimes we realize we have the confidence we need to learn and take risks. They are also iterative; we need to go through the Developing Process (as well as Discovering and Designing) over and over in our lives. It is by going through these processes time and again that we truly transform ourselves and develop into the person we most want to become. That is how we learn to live a passionate life.

Key #3—Risking

An important time in my life when I had to do something so different was in December 1976 when I quit a job with the federal government just before Christmas. I had just turned 33 years old and I had a family. I had small children, a three-year-old son and a 6-month-old daughter. I was married and my wife worked as a nurse's aide but she did not earn very much. My income had been the major source of our survival. I had a mortgage payment and an auto loan payment to make each month as well as utilities, food, and clothing expenses. My relatives and in-laws thought I was doing all the right things in life by keeping a job and taking care of the family. . . . At work there was too much to do and the pay was not that good given the inflationary conditions. Advancement to better salary and benefits became a problem because I was classified as a special appointment and I could not advance beyond it. Work became a tedious job. . . . I began to make errors which I normally would not make. In the autumn of 1976 I got tired of it all and I concluded that I could do better in another place and doing something else so I gave my two weeks notice one week before Christmas. . . . I had to do something else, that was my passion. I had to find my way to a better and more satisfying career. I did not know what it was but I was going to find it.

—FRANK MORGAN, **Native American educator**

Risk is an essential part of living passionately. Everyone we talked to told us about the risk-taking that was necessary to find his or her passion. Some of our interviewees took huge risks, and others took smaller ones, but all took risks. Some described it as facing challenges, overcoming obstacles, trying new ideas, or making changes. Whatever the terminology, it all relates to taking risks. You cannot find and live your passion without taking some risk. The risk may be finding out what is important to you, trying new options, or learning new things.

Risk is synonymous with danger, peril, hazard, or taking a chance. It means venturing into unknown territory or jumping into the deep end. It means taking what is safe and making it vulnerable.

Risk-taking is very hard for many people. They do not want to jeopardize their families, chance financial ruin, or face terra incognita. At work we are often penalized for taking risks. All risk-taking should be done prudently and with much thought. However, if you find yourself in a job you hate or if you work in a draining environment, you may choose to take some large risks.

> People who once thought it risky to leave a seemingly secure job to pursue what they really want are beginning to realize that, today, it is at least as risky *not* to identify and follow their dreams. They understand that they need to take a more proactive approach to career—that they are ill-advised to leave their fate in their employer's hands. They recognize the need to be creatively involved in designing, crafting, and shaping their own careers *before* they reach a state of crisis—economic or otherwise. (Boldt 1996: 30)

Facing risks is inevitable. Everyone has experienced risk-taking and knows they will probably face it many times in the future. Some people seek out risky situations whereas others are risk-aversive. Despite the fact that everyone knows what a risk is, the definitions of risk are extremely ambiguous. Risk has been defined as "a chance of loss" (Slovic 1964: 220), "the difference between your reach and your grasp" (Byrd 1974: 10), "a decision situation, involving choice among alternatives, which is characterized by a lack of certainty and the prospect of loss or failure" (Kogan and Wallach 1967: 113), "the likelihood, or probability, of some adverse effect of a hazard," and as "the probability of some future event" (Short 1984: 711). In a review of risk-taking in decisionmaking, Rapoport and Wallsten state "the concept of risk is psychologically meaningful but highly elusive" (1972: 145).

Risk and Motivation

Risk-taking has been studied by social scientists for over fifty years. Theories have come and gone, tests and measures have been tried and failed. Defining the construct of risk has proven elusive and made testing and theorizing about it very difficult. Once it was thought there was a personality trait that could be extracted and labeled "risk propensity." When this trait could not be found, researchers began to study risk-taking in specific situations. Again, they met with failure. Risk was so difficult to pin down it seemed that even specific risk situations could not be cornered and described. What has emerged is an agreement that risk-taking depends on the perception of the individual (Boverie 1988).

Boverie (1988) developed a multidimensional model of risk-taking based on motive, decision-making, and type of risk. In this model, risks were categorized into physical, ethical, interpersonal, occupational, and monetary risks. A relationship was found between these different kinds of risk and the level of decision-making involved. This research found that risks involving occupational choice were generally well thought out. Individuals were less likely to make rash decisions in this area and fewer occupational risks were actually taken here than in other parts of life. A person is more likely to take a physical risk, for example, than an occupational risk.

Examining our livelihood and making changes has profound consequences on our lives. For most people, things have to be pretty bad or the opportunities have to be very good for us to make a dramatic move from one job to another, from one employer to another. Many people are complacent enough to spend most of their waking hours doing work they find uninteresting, mundane, and unfulfilling. We are not willing to change unless the motive for change is great or the change is foisted upon us.

We take risks when we are highly motivated to change something in our lives. Maslow's Hierarchy of Needs model (1954)helps us to examine the relationship of motivation to drive. Maslow asserts that we will be motivated to seek that which we need, be it survival, social, or self-actualization needs. There is also research that links drive and passion to success. "In one study, for instance, educational psychologist Benjamin Bloom examined the lives of some of America's most accomplished artists, athletes, and scientists. He discovered that drive and determination, not great natural talent, led to their success in their respective fields" (HH Dalai Lama and Cutler 1998: 228).

Organizations have studied motivation for economic purposes. McGregor's Theory X and Y (1960), Herzberg's Hygiene Model (1967), and the Expectancy and Valance Model (Vroom 1964) are all examples of different motivational theories that have come out of organizational studies. Most of the current literature focuses now on the universal principle that humans are uniquely different and that one theory cannot explain motivation. Schein (1997) suggests that we need to look instead at the changes in the individual's life cycle and at their social conditions. We should, he says, rely on the ability of people to learn how to change and grow in the direction they want to go. Schein points out that the incentive and control systems in most organizations are built on either old or simplistic assumptions about human nature, which are not even shared by all.

> If members of a given organization have different assumptions about the nature of work activity and its relative importance to other activities, those differences will manifest themselves in frustration and communication breakdowns. (Schein 1997: 130)

Risk and Learning

We can learn how to take risks. You should begin with incremental steps—first taking smaller risks that have little consequence and then as you develop a comfort with risk-taking you can progress to larger risks. One woman told us of her love for singing but also of her fear of doing it in public. She had to learn how to control her fear so she could take the risk of performing.

I sang at church, tried out for things at school that I never would have gone near without music spurring me on. . . . I learned to mask the shaking limbs and quivery voice that my nerves produced, to stop looking at my shoes and to take the frozen pained look off my face while singing. Only someone severely in love [with what they were doing] would endure the pain and misery I went through.

There is an excitement, an energy that comes with expanding ourselves. It requires us to get outside of our normal comfort zone.

Living creatively and courageously requires us to get outside of our comfort zones. We need to be comfortable being uncomfortable, balancing on the very edge of losing control, of failure, of not understanding what we are doing. It is out there that discoveries are made and lives are fully lived. (Wilson and Wilson 1998: 162)

Eileen Allison, the educational consultant we have mentioned before, told us how she took the progressively risky steps that led to her current passion for work.

A principal's job came up in the area. I applied for it. But then I heard about another job opening up in a regional education agency. This job, "Director of School Improvement," really enticed me . . . but it would not open for application until the principal position would close. So, feeling on one hand that I should go for the "bird in the hand"—I applied for the principal position and was offered it.

Immediately, I became nagged by an inner voice that said to reject the principal position, take the risk, and apply for the Director position when it became available. I could not sleep at night because this voice was so strong. So, I turned down the principal's position and waited.

I rationalized: "Heck, you already have risked so much why come this far and then take the safe road?"

The happy news is I was offered the director's position. This ended up being one of the best decisions of my life. Not only did I earn more money, but a whole world of new challenges and opportunity came my way, launching me into better paying positions and incredible learning.

. . . Here is my point in all this: For me, once I had risked so much already, instead of scrambling to safer ground when the first job came along, I decided what the hell, I don't have much to lose. Go for the job you really want.

Organizations can be very helpful in supporting this kind of risk-taking behavior. There are organizations that punish employees who take risks, whereas others allow risk and support employees who take risks routinely. When we stop stretching ourselves, we begin to die a little. The same thing happens with organizations. If employees are not encouraged to try new things, to make mistakes, and to go beyond the ordinary, they will become the living dead. Managers and supervisors can exemplify prudent risk-taking, as well as encourage employees to correct work problems on their own or to develop cost-saving suggestions for their areas. Most people who don't take risks have had the behavior drummed out of them through negative reinforcement. If we want employees to take more initiative on the job, we need to encourage and reward them. People who take risks are constantly learning—about themselves and about their work.

Key #4—Learning

Now the things that used to interfere with learning no longer do, because I am in a more mature stage . . . and have learned how to handle certain situations better. I do have some fear of learning new things but I try to turn the fear into excitement; or I try to turn the fear into a strong motivational force. . . . I have learned to save money. . . . I have also learned to set a goal months in advance about what I need to invest in. . . . There are some negative past experiences related to learning and recording music, but I try to learn everything I can from negative experiences. Overall, "positive" past experiences have played a very strong role in my continuing to write music and learn new things.

—PAUL PINO, musician and educator

At the deeper level, this [passionate] experience encouraged me to make meaning from my experience—a highly personal and emotional task. I recall many moments in the production process where my notes went by the wayside to allow the fluid creative process to take hold. Sometimes that meant I faced emotions about my own life experience that I would rather not have confronted. But had I limited the art, I would have limited the outcomes—for me, the creative team and the audiences that came.

—SHAWN SHEPHERD, **theater director**

Passionate people are always learning, reinventing themselves, and exploring new things. You must be learning in your job to have passion. If you aren't, you need to either find new things to learn or move on to something new.

After we have taken risks, it is important that we learn from the experience. We need to learn, first of all, that we can take risks. Second, we need to learn the lesson that the risk taught us. Frank Morgan, the person who quit his job just before Christmas, told us, "I was very passionate about getting through the psychology degree program to which I had committed myself. I had a philosophy statement: learning and completing the program was just as necessary as breathing. I commuted 180 miles a day to get to classes from home, even in the winter when the roads got snow packed. I took my children to the campus with me every day." Learning for him was just as necessary as breathing! What a lesson to learn.

The Dalai Lama tells us about the connection between learning and happiness:

> "So, the first step in seeking happiness is learning" (1998: 38). He goes on to say, "So, through this process of learning, of analyzing which thoughts and emotions are beneficial and which are harmful, we gradually develop a firm determination to change, feeling, 'Now the secret to my own happiness, my own good future, is within my own hands, I must not miss that opportunity!'" (HH Dalai Lama and Cutler 1998: 38)

Individual Learning

The literature on lifelong learning and adult learning in particular emphasizes experiential and transformational learning theory. Malcolm

Knowles (1973) developed a theory of adult learning that he called Andragogy. Andragogy has the following six-core adult learning principles:

- Adults need to know. The world is ever changing and to keep up, adults must be life-long learners. They need to know what they need to learn and what they need to do in order to learn.
- The self-concept of the learner is vital to his or her learning. Adults can learn through self-direction and in an autonomous fashion. Prior learning experience either in school or the workplace has a great effect on one's belief in the ability to learn.
- The role of the learner's experiences is also very important. Adults have a wealth of life experiences upon which to draw as resources and to use as mental models.
- Adults have a readiness to learn. They want to learn things that are life related and have significance for their day-to-day work and life.
- The adults have a problem-centered approach to learning. They also need and like to learn in a contextual setting that provides them hands-on experience.
- Adults are motivated to learn from the expected payoff of the effort and/or the intrinsic value of the learning. They don't want to learn something they can't use or is of no interest to them.

David Kolb (1984) has been a leader in the field of experiential learning. From Knowles's work we know that adults prefer learning that is experiential and active. Adults do not take well to sitting at desks all day listening to a trainer. They prefer to learn by doing and thinking. But one can't learn by doing alone. Reflection and internalization are necessary components for deep learning. Kolb created the experiential learning cycle that includes all of these learning activities:

- Concrete experience—the full involvement in here-and-now experiences;
- Observations and reflection—reflection on and observation of the learner's experiences from many perspectives;

- Formation of abstract concepts and generalization—the creation of concepts that integrate the learners' observations into logically sound theories; and
- Testing implications of new concepts in new situations—using these theories to make decisions and solve problems.

Kolb's work provided a theoretical basis for experiential learning and a practical model for the learning process.

Perspective transformation, according to Mezirow (1981), has a critical effect on how and why adults learn. He feels that adults develop by examining their underlying assumptions and beliefs in order to free themselves from the constraints of unproductive beliefs. This perspective transformation, as he calls it, is a learning process. It is a way for adults to reexamine their lives and to take action to overcome culturally defined dependency roles. According to Mezirow (2000), the most important outcome of transformational learning is adult growth. It is the process by which adults become who they are and how they make sense of themselves. The transformation process is about change that is central to adult development.

Transformational learning focuses on how individuals create meaning from their experiences, whether these are internal or external. Not all of our learning is transformational—training for new skills or simply adding new information to our schema is not usually considered transformational. Much of our most profound learning, however, is transformational.

Transformational learning relies on the process of critical reflection and meaning making. Transformation begins with a disorienting dilemma—an event that causes us to stop and reflect on life. When one stops to reflect, the process of self-examination occurs. Through self-examination we face our basic values, beliefs, assumptions, and feelings about ourselves. Once we have confronted our basic assumptions, asked ourselves if they are valid, and perhaps revised or rejected them, we then seek to understand how they fit with our view of the world. We seek to come to terms with our new meanings and check outside ourselves to see if they fit with others.

Living your passion and transformational learning cannot be separated and like the other processes in our model, they are iterative. Discovering your passion can happen through critical reflection. Likewise, it is difficult to follow your dreams unless you make a conscious effort to get there. Once you find you are living your dream, you must continue to develop and refine your world. Adult learning and transformational learning theories provide the means for individuals to move through the Passion Transformation Model.

Organizational Learning

The concept of organizational learning was first developed by Argyris and Schôn in 1978 and is considered today, more than ever, to be one of the most important arenas for organizational growth. Watkins and Marsick (1993) describe the concept of a learning organization:

> One that learns continuously and transforms itself. Learning takes place in individuals, teams, the organization, and even the communities with which the organization interacts. Learning is a continuous, strategically used process—integrated with, and running parallel to, work. Learning results in changes in knowledge, beliefs, and behaviors. Learning also enhances organizational capacity for innovation and growth. The learning organization has embedded processes to capture and share learning. (1993: 8–9)

Senge et al. describe a deep organizational learning cycle in which "team members develop new skills and capabilities which alter what they can do and understand. As new capabilities develop, so too do new awarenesses and sensibilities. Over time, as people start to see and experience the world differently, new beliefs and assumptions begin to form, which enables further development of skills and capabilities" (1994: 18). This cycle, they say, is the essence of the learning organization because it not only includes but also goes beyond capability development to include fundamental shifts of both individual and organizational mindsets.

Marquart says, "what organizations *know* takes second place to what and how quickly they can *learn*" (xvii). A learning organization "is an organization which learns powerfully and collectively and is continually transforming itself to better collect, manage, and use knowledge for corporate success" (Marquart 1996: 19).

Organizations can do much to foster adult transformation, learning, and growth. Workplaces that seek to become organizations that learn have as a core value the importance of learning. For an organization to learn, the individuals in the organization must first learn, and then the teams and work groups must learn from their individual members. Subsequently, the whole organization can adopt new practices.

> In a sense, not only is a true learning organization far beyond a traditional program of structured training, it is far beyond what many people think when they hear the term learning organization. In reality, it is a developing organization—developing individuals, interrelationships, teams, knowledge, wisdom, theory, and application. (Lucas 1999: 49)

Organizations that value learning are likely to provide ongoing training and education programs for all employees. Other programs that reinforce learning are tuition reimbursement, mentoring, and career development programs. Organizations need to provide the resources and the support needed to help employees develop and keep their passion. People who are constantly learning are more likely to be passionate and to feel confident about their abilities, thus helping organizations to thrive. Organizations as entities must also continue to learn and grow. Organizations that learn are continually evaluating their processes and decisionmaking to further their own organizational growth.

Key #5—Building Self-Efficacy

> Returning to school has helped me to begin to discover myself. I know that sounds "out there," but that is how I feel. Being in school has helped me to feel "free." I have taken the initiative to do things I thought I would never do, and I am learning to be assertive and tell those I love, "This is who I am." I feel strong and empowered. I continue to have days in which I question my decision and wonder if I will ever know who I really am, but I am happy.
>
> —CHRISTINE COKER, special education teacher

Throughout this phase I have felt extremely motivated to learn and realize my full potential. My energy level is tremendous and my drive is unending. My brain is in overdrive due to the overwhelming number of stimulating and exciting things regularly happening that I process daily. I constantly feel as though life is handing me more and more opportunities. In conversations with my family, I tell them that I feel as though my life is too good to be true. There are daily ups and downs, but overall, my life is on a huge upswing. I feel that there is so much for me to learn and so many ways for me to apply my talents.

—CHELLE STRINGER, **school administrator**

I learned things about myself that had been hidden till that point. I could approach a group of people and have something to offer them and they would accept it. I could overcome fear and override the physical effects of it. I could pour out emotions in music that may have stayed bottled up till my midlife crisis. I was set free by this ability. It wasn't all roses—there were the times of self-doubt, notes that wouldn't come, music I didn't like, and music scores that wouldn't implant themselves in my head. That is the real beauty of a thing of passion, though—it doesn't always come easily. It makes you follow it carefully as well as with abandon. If it did not have some elusive properties you probably would not follow so closely.

—TRUDY CANDELARIA, **musician, speech pathologist**

Self-efficacy is the belief that we have about our ability to do something. It powerfully affects our behavior. As the stories told above by some of our interviewees demonstrate, self-efficacy frees them, it encourages them, and it makes life exciting and the sense of accomplishment greater. You may have the skills and talent to move up the ladder or take a promotion, but if you believe that you are not capable of being successful, you may not take advantage of opportunities presented to you. Positive self-efficacy is developed by trying things and then evaluating how you do. People with low self-efficacy are unlikely to try new things, and hence lead less passionate lives. One of the most important aspects about self-efficacy is that we can change it relatively easily, from low to high. Often, taking small steps builds self-efficacy over time.

Self-Efficacy Theory

Self-efficacy is a term coined by Albert Bandura (1982). He describes it as a person's sense of his or her ability to deal effectively with the environment. This self-assessment can have a profound effect on our choices and behaviors. When people think that they can perform a behavior, they are willing to engage in activities requiring such behavior. People with high self-efficacy are willing to put forth substantial effort to master challenges, take risks, and persist in the face of obstacles. When individuals think that they cannot successfully perform, they are not willing to engage in activities, may slacken their effort, settle for less or mediocre outcomes, and quit in the face of obstacles (Bandura 1989).

Efficacy expectations come from four sources: direct experience, vicarious experience, verbal persuasion, and our physiological state (Bandura 1989). Direct experience is the most influential source of efficacy. We believe what we experience. If we fail at something, we are less likely to try it again. If we succeed at something, we are more likely to do it again. Watching others succeed or fail also influences us. This is called vicarious learning, and it depends on how similar the person being observed is to yourself. Coaches, teachers, and parents have long known the influence of verbal persuasion. A good pep talk to a team that is losing has made all the difference in their expectations and behaviors. Finally, our physiological state can influence our efficacy expectations. Feeling lousy negatively influences our belief in whether we can accomplish a goal and feeling great positively influences our belief in our ability.

Self-efficacy is a construct that has evolved out of social cognitive theory. A central tenet of this theory is that one's ability to store symbolic information in memory permits an individual to anticipate the consequences of his or her actions, to then set goals and plan steps to meet the expected consequences, and finally, to weigh evidence from different sources to assess his or her own capabilities (Bandura 1986). Therefore, self-efficacy refers to a person's judgments about his or her own capability to perform at a given level.

What is critical about Bandura's theory is the relationship between the individual and his environment. Behavior becomes a function of the interaction between the two. How we think about ourselves will affect how we behave. The information we receive from the outside world also affects how we think about ourselves.

Building self-efficacy is similar to a self-fulfilling prophecy. If we believe we can do it, we are more likely to do it. If we believe we can't do it, we probably won't even try. Thus, being able to take the risk to live your life more passionately depends largely on your efficacy level. In his book *How to Find the Work You Love,* Boldt writes:

> While they may accept that it is a good idea for others, many people doubt that it is really possible for them to earn a living doing the work they love. Whether or not it will be possible for you depends, in a large measure, on whether or not you believe it is possible for you. What you believe will shape what you do and don't do. It will shape the opportunities you attract or don't attract. It will determine whether or not you can recognize opportunities when they do come along and what you do with them. One thing is for sure, if you don't believe you can, the chances that you ever will are next to nil. (1996: 31)

Self-Efficacy and Learning

Learning something new is a powerful way to increase your efficacy level. Every time we learn, our efficacy goes up, and our attitudes change.

Self-efficacy is different from self-esteem. Self-esteem refers to one's sense of self-worth. Self-efficacy is malleable, in that we can change it relatively easily from low to high. Having one little success, or taking a class, or working with an expert can change one's level of efficacy about work rather quickly. Self-esteem, on the other hand, is a durable feature of one's life. If someone's self-esteem is low, it will take more than just a small success to change it. It takes years to form an individual's self-esteem and it takes years to change it. The interesting relationship between them is that even if you have low self-esteem, you can have high self-efficacy about your ability to perform. Conversely, a tennis player may have high self-esteem but low efficacy about playing golf or developing a strategic plan for an organization. Learning can affect our self-efficacy and one's level of self-efficacy can affect his or her belief about the ability to learn.

Organizations can help develop self-efficacy in their employees by providing training and opportunities to try new things in a safe environment. Knowing that making mistakes when doing something new will not be held against them can help employees stretch and grow. Organizations can provide safe places to learn new skills, try them out, and reward employees for the new learning. This will increase the efficacy of the employees to continue learning.

By taking either little or big steps, we are taking *risks,* as we risk we *learn,* and as we learn we develop higher *self-efficacy,* our belief that we can accomplish what we set out to do. All three, working together, advance our quest for a more passionate life. The relationship of risk, learning, and self-efficacy is vitally important to transforming one's life and to living passionately.

We believe that these concepts take what we currently know about motivating people at work and expand our knowledge by providing useful and practical methods to help people find more fulfillment through work. Practicing the five keys to passionate work—discovering, creating, risking, learning, and building self-efficacy—leads to Occupational Intimacy . . . and passion. The result is what one person we talked to described as "Lighting up from the inside. Aliveness. Transcendence. Feeling totally present and absorbed. Joy. Wonder. Moving, inspiring, resonating, vibrating."

In the next chapter we send out a call to action. Will you accept the challenge to find your passion? Can you help your organization to create environments where individuals can find passionate work?

EXERCISE FOURTEEN: Developing—Individual

Developing is the "putting it into action" process. It has three critical subprocesses that are Risking, Learning, and Building Self-Efficacy. These processes are continual and interactive. They are important separately and jointly. This exercise is intended to make you more aware of how you relate to these three important activities.

Learning

What is your preferred learning style? Do like to learn by jumping into activities and doing them yourself? By watching how others do things? By reflecting upon experiences? By theorizing or conceptualizing?

What motivates you to learn?

What is holding you back from learning?

Risking

Do you consider yourself in general as more of a risk taker or as someone who is risk averse? Why?

We know that people are more willing to take risks in certain parts of their lives than in others. Which areas of your life are you more willing to take risk? Which areas are you less willing?

What would stop you from taking a risk? What would cause you to be more of a risk taker?

Building Self-Efficacy

Do you believe that you are capable of achieving work that is passionate? Why or why not?

What would it take for you to feel capable? We know that self-efficacy can be build by taking tiny steps and then ever larger steps. What steps will you take?

EXERCISE FIFTEEN: Developing—Organizations

Developing is the "putting it into action" process. It has three critical subprocesses that are Risking, Learning, and Building Self-Efficacy. These processes are continual and interactive. They are important separately and jointly. This exercise is intended to make you more aware of how your organization supports these three important activities.

Learning

Are you insuring that employees are continually learning on the job? How or why not? How could you improve?

Does your organization value organizational learning? How does it demonstrate this? How could it improve?

Risking

Do you encourage employee risk-taking?

What are the incentives or penalties for employees to try new things?How much does your organization encourage employees to learn from their mistakes?

When is the last time your senior leaders took risks, admitted mistakes of their own, and found ways for the company to learn from them?

Building Self-Efficacy

Do you believe that your organization is capable of creating a passionate work environment? Why or why not?

What would it take for you to feel capable? We know that self-efficacy can be build by taking tiny steps and then ever larger steps. What steps will you take to develop your organizational efficacy?

Do you feel your employees are capable of being passionate about their work? If not, why do you keep them? If so, are you doing everything you can to help them create passion around their work? What else could your organization do to make a big difference for employees in this area?

Transforming Work:
The Five Keys to Achieving
Trust, Commitment, and
Passion in the Workplace

In the prologue of this book we talked about our stories and described what led us to write this book and to do research on the transformational power of passion. Although the events in our lives had a great impact on us, it has been the stories of our study participants and the many hundreds of others to whom we have talked in workshops and presentations that fires our passion for working on this topic and continues to transform us personally. Some of these stories have made us cry, some have made us angry, and some left us in awe. Every one of them taught us something.

The process of conducting this research and writing this book has been an exciting adventure, filled with both perils and triumphs. We have learned so much about ourselves. We had to face our own demons, to try to follow our own advice, and to walk our own talk. Because we believe so fervently in the power of our Passion Transformation Model we could deal better with the difficult and challenging issues in our own lives. What makes us confident is that our model is based not on suppositions, but upon the voices and experiences of hundreds of working adults. *They* told us how they found passionate work. *They* told us how they lost their interest in work. *They* told us of their transformational work experiences. We took these stories, extracted the data, and compared what we found to conventional work motivation theories. When the data didn't fit those theories, we delved deeper, and asked ourselves, "What were they really saying?" Our theory, that passion for work follows a similar sequence and constructs as relationship development and theories of love and attachment, was confirmed by their stories.

It makes so much sense. Loving what you do is so very much like loving another person. You have to basically like the person/work, you have to be able to stay the course with that person/work, you have to give as well as get from that person/work, you have to trust, honor, and find that person/work meaningful to you, and the person/work must keep your interest, your care, and your devotion. We all search for and sometimes find that person to whom we can devote ourselves; likewise, we all search for and sometimes find that occupation to which we can devote ourselves.

Passion suggests strong feelings, feelings that reside deep within ourselves. We are passionate about those people and things that stir those feelings, that touch our basic values and beliefs. When we connect, reflect, and are in touch with those basic values and beliefs, then we can transform our lives. We can make the choices that before seemed hard or impossible to do. When we discover, truly discover, what is important to us, then we can formulate the plans to live the lives that are meaningful to ourselves. When we are doing meaningful, interesting work in organizations that care about that work, then we become capable of steering our own course and living passionate lives.

Leadership and Passion

The first, and indispensable, requirement for creating passionate organizations is for its leaders to be passionate themselves. Paul Shirley and two other founders created SVS, Inc. Starting in 1993 with no employees, $3,000, and a dream, SVS was sold to the Boeing Company on July 9, 2000, as one of the premier technology companies in the world. Today, SVS is a world-class leader in directed energy pointing and tracking systems. "We started with something *we* loved to do," Shirley explains. "If you start with that foundation—the leaders of the company—you have a serious shot at making a passionate workplace," he says. "I was willing to sacrifice just about anything."

Tom Peters, writing in the March 2001 issue of *Fast Company,* says:

Leaders wear their passion on their sleeves. There's absolutely no question in my mind. . . . Leadership, in the end, is all about having energy, creating energy, showing energy, and spreading energy. Leaders emote, they erupt, they flame, and they have boundless (nutty) enthusiasm. And why should-n't they? The cold logic of it is unassailable: If you do not love what you are doing, if you do not go totally bonkers for your project, your team, your customers, and your company, then why in the world are you doing what you are doing? And why in the world would you expect anybody to follow you? (136)

Warren Bennis said, "I have never met a great leader without passion. Many leaders are rather soft-spoken, but when they talk they are passionate" (1998: 5). Jack Welch, the hard-nosed leader of General Electric, once said:

The CEO succession here is still a long way off, but I think about it every day. Obviously, anybody who gets this job must have a vision for the company and be capable of rallying people behind it. He or she has got to be very comfortable in a global environment, dealing with world leaders. Be comfortable dealing with people at all levels of the company. Have a boundaryless attitude toward every constituency—race, gender, every-thing. Have the very highest standards of integrity. Believe in the gut that people are the key to everything, and that change is not something you fear—it's something you relish. Anyone who is too inwardly focused who doesn't cherish customers, who isn't open to change isn't going to make it. (Tichy and Sherman 1993: 250)

Trying to create a passionate organization without having passionate leaders is like trying to start a car without gas—you just can't. Passionate leaders create an inspiring vision of the future, deeply understand the importance of what the organization does and how it affects customers and other publics, and then find ways to connect those to the feelings, hopes, and plans of their employees. Passionate leaders find ways to in-still and draw out passion in people at all levels of the company. If you are a leader without passion for your own work and for your organization, it is time to think deeply about what is important to you and why, and it can't be simply making money. If you can't reclaim that passion, it is time to move on. You owe it to yourself and to the employees who count on you for leadership.

The primary role of top management is to lead the organization. Leaders must consider the best means for steering the company and for developing products and services that will keep the organization productive and prosperous. Since organizations are made up of people—of employees—then the leader's responsibility is to lead the people of their organization. As organizational consultants, we work with leaders to help them solve their problems. In many cases, the biggest problems these leaders face are those dealing with their workforce. Leaders tell us "they are not motivated, they have a morale problem, they are not able to make decisions, correct problems, or don't have the skills and expertise to do the work."

There are many, many books that propose solutions to these "people" problems. These resources give wonderful advice and talk about companies that have found success. Hearing about successful businesses is motivating but when we look at our own organizations we realize that our resources, programs, environment, or history are barriers to achieving the success of these "excellent" organizations.

So beyond having passion for your work and organization, what can you do to lead your organization? How can you create an organization where people are motivated, happy, competent, and productive? As you know, the answers are not simple or easy, nor can they be corrected with short-term "Band-Aids.'" Just as personal change is hard, unsettling, disruptive, and uncertain, so is organizational change. But it is only through systemic, holistic, well-thought-out change that sustainable growth can happen. You've seen the damage that short-term solutions have caused. Employees are tired of flavor-of-the-month programs. They tell newcomers, "Yeah, we tried that five years ago and it didn't work then, and it won't work now." When faced with "new" programs or reorganizations, employees regress, revolt, and retreat.

One of the reasons that some attempts at organizational change are unsuccessful is that employees know that the change is being implemented for the "good" of the company, but at their expense. Leaders are faced with looking at bottom lines, at P & L statements, at quarterly and year-end financials. When faced with numbers that need to be changed, a sure method for fixing the numbers is to play with other numbers. Reorganizing, cost cutting, or increasing production will have a positive effect on the numbers leaders must contend with—for a while. But short-term solutions tend to have long-term systemic effects. This is not to say that some of these changes are not necessary, just that the long-term effects of the changes must be taken into account when they are considered.

As a leader, it is your responsibility to look forward, backward, and deep inside. You must know where you want the organization to go, where the organization has been, and its strengths and weaknesses. You need to know more than just day-to-day operations—you must be able to forecast year-to-year progress. You need to understand how the organization operates, when it is healthy, when it is sick, what it needs to grow, and what keeps it from developing. Because the basic building block of your organization is the people who work there, you must understand them, their issues, what makes them come to work, what will keep them working, and then be prepared to set the course to correct or realign systemic barriers to their growth.

If your halls are filled with the living dead, if your best employees are being hired away, or if you can't seem to hire highly motivated and trained employees, then you need to look at what your organization is doing to thwart itself. In this book you have read what hundreds of working adults have said about finding passionate work and workplaces. They want an organization to care about the work they do. They want to do meaningful work. They want to enjoy the work and the work environment. Does your organization truly care about the effort each employee makes each day? Do you, personally, care about them? Does your organization structure jobs so that they are interesting? Do your employees know why and just how important the work they are doing is to the organization? To society? Are people smiling, happy, and excited to come to work? Does your organization promote fun and joy at work? Do supervisors and managers care about the personal issues of their employees? These are some of the things that people told us makes them motivated to work. How does your organization stack up?

We have known for years that employees enjoy work and work harder if they are treated well. In 1957, Douglas McGregor gave us Theory Y and why we should treat employees as motivated, self-directed people. We also have known for years that interesting work and a nice environment is important to motivation. Herzberg, in 1968, told us all about hygiene and motivating factors. So why are employees still unhappy and unmotivated? What makes them feel passionately about their work? We found that along with having a nice, caring place to work, doing meaningful work, and being treated as responsible adults—employees want to learn. We found that continuous learning and growth in an area employees find meaningful increases their love for the work itself, their enthusiasm for coming to work, and helps them to find fulfillment through their work.

The answer then, in a nutshell, is for leaders to construct workplaces where not only the environments and benefits are good, where jobs are challenging and interesting, and where employees know why they are important, but also where they have opportunities to learn and develop. Learning, taking risks, and the subsequent effect that has upon employee self-efficacy is what keeps them on the payroll, keeps them passionate, and keeps the organization learning, growing, and prospering. Constructing these workplaces requires nothing short of transforming work. Leadership is where the transformation process must start.

Transforming Work

The title of this book, *Transforming Work,* carries two meanings. Transforming work can mean the act of changing the work itself, so that it can be more enjoyable, meaningful, and productive. Both individuals and organizations can act to transform work in this sense. Alternatively, transforming work can mean work that changes the individual. In this instance, the work environment or the tasks involved in completing the work act on the individual to transform him or her into someone, preferably, who is increasingly growing, learning, and enthusiastic. In this book we have focused on both the individual and the organizational transformation required to work with passion.

Personal transformation is a complex undertaking. Although we have tried to provide guidance throughout this book, no book can take the place of our own personal wisdom or the personal care and support of others. In *Effective Teaching and Mentoring: Realizing the Transforma-*

tional Power of Adult Learning Experiences, Laurent Daloz says, "Students can be powerfully affected by their teachers. Many of us carry memories of an influential teacher who may scarcely know we existed, yet who said something at just the right time in our lives to snap a whole world into focus" (1986: 21). He says that:

> For each of us, tangled inside our own stories, the endings are hidden. Yet most of us spend the better part of our lives trying to assure ourselves that our tales are already told, even if not yet lived, and that they have a happy ending. The discovery that this might not be so can, in itself, lead to a profound transformation. But the appearance of someone who has already taken the journey can bring a sigh of relief to the best of us. That is where mentors come in. They have been there before, and we greet them with awe and, above all, hope. (27)

Each person reading this book will have the opportunity to mentor others—as a friend, coach, leader, or spouse—along the road to passionate work. In that sense you will be transforming work yourself, for another. Interestingly, passion itself is what will make you a good guide. "The recognition that passion is central to learning and the capacity to provide emotional support when it is needed are hallmarks that distinguish the good mentor from the mediocre teacher," Daloz says (33).

Transformation is scary; it means loss in addition to gain, and it means taking risks. Sometimes it involves transforming the work to meet your needs, and sometimes it means transforming yourself to reach the work you love. And what are we looking for? Daloz provides a clue:

> Yet at the end of the journey lies a new identity. Traveled with integrity, the way home leads to a fuller and clearer sense of who we are, a new and broader boundary between oneself and the world. The struggle to be something more than the person others have made, to construct and then live up to a set of our own expectations, is one of the most compelling struggles of our adult lives. (1986: 154)

As we seek work that we can be passionate about we will be transformed. The very process of seeking changes us from what we were to something else. The act of setting goals and developing skills and knowledge changes us from what we were to something else. Make no mistake—you are on a journey of personal transformation.

Organizational transformation is also a complex undertaking that requires the people in the organization to change, as well as the organization itself. Many of our organizational cultures are currently based on assumptions that have gone unquestioned since the early part of the twentieth century. "In the workplace, stagnant and oppressive organizational conditions persist simply because of the unquestioning acceptance of traditional organizational norms" (Brookfield 1990: 147). These very assumptions are the starting place for organizational transformation.

For organizational transformation to occur, all members of the organization must (1) be free to question assumptions and beliefs and (2) work together to create a new system based on clear assumptions, values, and beliefs. In the Passion Transformation Model the Discovery process provides for systematic exploration of organizational assumptions, values, beliefs, and barriers that are the foundation of the current culture. It is in examining these basic systems of belief that an organization can begin the process for transforming work.

Understanding the barriers to a passionate workplace is only the beginning step. Once dysfunctional assumptions or beliefs are uncovered, leaders must work with their employees to create new or more developed organizational cultures. The research on organizational culture tells us that it is the leaders' values and beliefs that drive the culture (Schein 1992). But it is the employees who must work and live within the culture. Most organizational cultures were not created systematically or with a specific design in mind. Because of this, many cultures have dysfunctional aspects that inhibit employee development and passion for work. Working with employees to transform the organization will help to ensure that the new workplace is one where the employees can develop and grow.

Because learning is so vital to passionate employees, opportunities for learning must be carefully and systemically integrated into the organizational structure, processes, and procedures. Mentorship programs, adequate training for all job skills, leadership succession, formalized employee feedback, career development, tuition reimbursement, and

TABLE 8.1   Processes Enabling Organizational Transformation

- Understanding Adult Learning
- Engaging in Organizational Discourse
- Identifying Organizational Barriers
- Providing Forums For Critical Reflection
- Valuing Employee Input
- Establishing New Communication Networks
- Eliciting Stories of Experience
- Identifying Sources of Learning
- Ensuring Supportive Leadership
- Allowing Risk-taking
- Crossing Traditional Barriers

---

applications such as just-in-time training are but a few ways to help ensure that employees have opportunities for continual learning.

Not only must individual learning be accommodated, but also systems for organizational learning must be determined. Annual review of programs, opportunities for dialogue, knowledge preservation, and knowledge management systems are just a few systemic means for enhancing organizational learning. Table 8.1 contains suggestions of tools to use for the process of organizational transformation and learning.

Implementation of these new learning systems, processes, and procedures comprises the Developing Process. Inherent in development is trying out new things, revising what doesn't work, or coming up with new plans. For the development of a transformed workplace, allowances must be made for employees to take the risk of trying out new systems, processes, and procedures. It is by trying something that one learns the best—either because it succeeded or because it failed. Failure is often our best teacher. It increases our resilience. It helps us to anticipate future problems and opportunities. It forces us to develop an ability to look at different alternatives. If employees are reprimanded for either taking risks or for failing, learning can actually be stifled. It is through taking risks that employees learn and build self-efficacy about their abilities. This promotes a motivated workplace. Motivated employees trust their leaders and the organization, are more committed to organizational goals, and are passionate about their work.

Trust

Self-Trust

In *The Artist's Way*, Julia Cameron says, "Each of us has an inner dream that we can unfold if we will just have the courage to admit what it is. And the faith to trust our own admission" (1992: 193). Following what Campbell calls your "bliss" (1988: 113) is to trust what you believe to lay within yourself. Nathaniel Branden says, "To trust one's mind and to know that one is worthy of happiness is the essence of self-esteem" (1994: 4). The more we trust ourselves—our judgments and our feelings—the more likely we will take the risks involved in finding and creating passionate work for ourselves. The higher our self-efficacy, the more trust we have in our ability to do what we attempt to do. As we take risks, learn, and build self-efficacy—what we call the Developing process—we develop more trust in ourselves. We believe in ourselves, in our ability to overcome failure, and to make wise decisions.

Trust in Others

Organizations with high Occupational Intimacy have high levels of trust. Consider Senge et al., talking about the importance of intimacy in learning organizations:

> While intimacy offers a rich sense of involvement, it also implies vulnerability. . . . In intimate situations, you must be trustworthy, because you know that you are bound to your team in the long run by your shared purpose. The lack of trust pervasive in most organizations is not a *cause* of lack of intimacy, but a symptom of it. (1994: 71)

Transforming work to be more intimate, the workplace to be more nurturing, and employees to be more passionate increases trust. *Webster's* (1990) uses the following words to define trust: firm belief in the honesty, reliability of another; faith; confident expectation, or hope. Establishing trust is something that takes time, effort, and intention. Trust is transactional—it happens between one or more persons. Trust starts with oneself. To earn the trust of another one must first be trustworthy. Being trustworthy, according to Covey (1989), means keeping commitments, apologizing when you make mistakes, clarifying expectations, being loyal to those who aren't present, and providing little kindnesses and courtesies. Organizations wishing to build trust will first exercise trustworthiness. That means that leaders, in particular, must act with integrity.

Trust is one of our basic needs in life. Erik Erikson (1959) described trust as the first psychosocial crisis we deal with in our developmental process. If we fail to trust our caretakers as infants, we may have difficulty trusting others the rest of our lives. "Trust (or mistrust) is grounded in an affection that informs cognition" (Parks 2000: 32). Trust affects both our thoughts and our emotions.

In the workplace, trust is important for many reasons. If employees don't trust themselves, then they are less likely to take risks, to have high self-esteem, to develop trusting relationships with others, or to stretch themselves in order to grow. If employees have little trust for one another, they are less likely to share information, train others, take risks, or develop good working relationships. If employees have little trust for management, they are less likely to take risks, work toward organizational goals, apply themselves, and may even work to sabotage the organization. If management has little trust in employees, they do not allow opportunities for employee growth, allow employees to express themselves, to take risks, or even enjoy the work. Management will micromanage, dominate, and even oppress their employees. Our capacity to trust affects our ability to try new things, to care deeply about others, and our outlook on life.

Many of our organizations incorporate teams into their structures. The core building block to successful teams is trust. Without trust between the team members the team will usually fail. Again we find the connection to the literature on love and attachment. In a close relationship such as a marriage, trust is paramount. If trust is broken, the relationship begins to dissolve. This is also true of close friendships. When a trust is betrayed between friends, the relationship suffers.

Trusting itself can be transformational. When one offers her complete trust to another, she expects honesty and agreement on the terms of the relationship, whether those terms are implied or expressed. In giving over oneself completely to another, you are transforming your world to accept another into it. You must learn new ways of dealing with issues, with relationships, with yourself. In their book, *Trust and Betrayal in the Workplace*, Reina and Reina state:

> In work environments where transformative trust unfolds, individuals learn to work constructively with their need for power and control. They learn to manage their assumptions and fears and their need to protect their positions and expertise. The capacity to trust in relationships between individuals, among teams, and across the organization expands. (1999: 155)

Employees with high Occupational Intimacy trust. They trust management and their coworkers—because management and their coworkers have proven themselves trustworthy. They have provided a passionate work environment, a place of nurturance and care. Employees with high Occupational Intimacy seek opportunities to work hard for organizational goals because they know they will ultimately be the benefactors. They develop relationships with others in the organization that makes working there enjoyable. They develop confidence in their ability to do their work, contribute to the organization, and in their ability to develop.

If trust is present in organizations in all of its forms—within individuals, between individuals, and mutually between management and employees—all parties will benefit. Mutual trust between management and employees will lead to strong commitment to organizational goals, employee development, and prosperity of the organization.

Commitment

Perhaps Goethe said it best.

> Until one is committed, there is hesitancy, the chance to draw back, always ineffectiveness. Concerning all acts of initiative andcreation, there is one elementary truth the ignorance of which kills countless ideas and splendid plans: that the moment one definitely commits oneself, then providence moves too. All sorts of things occur to help one that would never otherwise have occurred. A whole stream of events issues from the decision, raising in one's favor all manner of unforeseen incidents, meetings and material

assistance which no man could have dreamed would have come his way. Whatever you can do or dream you can, begin it. Boldness has genius, power and magic in it. Begin it now.

Commitment implies a promise, vow, or understanding that you will follow through on your word. Keeping commitments is a foundation of trustworthiness and for building trust. Commitment is the glue that keeps trusting relationships together. Commitment is the extent to which someone is likely to stick with a situation or person.

Commitment implies a decision—an intentional decision. Commitment is found and is an important aspect of the theories of love and attachment. In Sternberg's Triangle of Love model (1987), commitment is one of the three components that make up love.

In Sternberg's model, commitment has both a short-term and a long-term aspect. The short-term aspect is the decision to love someone. The long term is the decision to maintain the relationship. Commitment is the component that keeps a relationship together, whereas intimacy and passion make the relationship interesting and intense.

In the workplace, committed employees make the decision to stay with an organization through good times and bad. Commitment leads to loyalty, which is important to keeping organizations healthy. Organizational leaders often complain about the lack of loyalty in their employees. If employees feel committed to the organizations, this would evaporate as a concern. But organizations also need to be committed to employees. Commitment is a two-way street—one will be committed if someone else commits back. When employees feel that they are just numbers that can easily be replaced, their commitment to the organization will fade.

Some employees are less likely to be committed to an organization per se than they are to a particular line of work or to relationships with leaders, coworkers, or role models. Generation X employees in particular feel little loyalty to organizations. Creating Occupational Intimacy is the key to keeping these employees. Providing work that these employees can feel passionate about and an environment where they feel cared for and have built strong interpersonal relationships will build commitments that are not necessarily organizational but that result in employee retention and commitment to the job.

Organizations try to get loyalty by providing a paycheck. But money alone does not inspire commitment, and without commitment you will not have loyalty. People want to commit themselves to something that is meaningful to them, that inspires them, that is important to them. In order to get commitment from employees, organizations have to provide the vision, the inspiration, and the means of achieving something meaningful. If organizations want a loyal workforce, they must show their commitment by providing investment in the employees' development and effort.

Passion

This book is about passion and passionate work. Let us summarize the importance of passion for organizations. Peter Senge talks about the importance of passion. He says:

> Our traditional system of management, based on the purpose of maximizing the shareholders' return, is the most well-designed system imaginable to produce consistently mediocre results. Companies like VISA, Shell, Toyota, Scania, and Interface have found that the key to success is not obsessively measuring costs and profits—it's nurturing the passion, imagination, creativity, persistence, patience, caring and desire to contribute. If you don't have those soft, unmeasurable things, you will never have an enterprise that can be highly successful. These organizations are managing performance in a way that is more consistent with how nature works. (1999: 9)

Organizational and workplace transformation requires renewed passion. It requires employee excitement for what they do and for what the organization stands for. Passionate employees become inspirations to others and affect others with their enthusiasm.

Passion is what this book is about, what is it is trying to do. To help others find work they are passionate about, to help build passionate workplaces where people love what they do and love to come to work each day. Places where creativity flows, energy is high, and everyone flourishes.

Exploring Transformation and Passion: Metaphors

Transformation can be compared to the practice of alchemy. Alchemists tried to turn lead into gold. When you are involved in a transformation process, whether willingly or if it is forced on you, you are in the process of becoming—of taking what is lead in you and turning it into gold. In his book *The Alchemist,* Paulo Coelho writes:

> [that's why alchemy exists] So that everyone will search for his treasure, find it, and then want to be better than he was in his former life. . . . That's what alchemists do. They show that, when we strive to become better than we are, everything around us becomes better, too. (1988: 151)

The Passion Transformation Model can help turn dispassionate employees and workplaces from being leaden people and places into motivated people who work in exciting caring organizations. Turn lead into gold.

Another metaphor for passion and how it affects one's life is that of a river. One of our interviewees, the Reverend Marianne Mcpherson, used a river metaphor to describe how passion has played a role in her life.

> Passion has been one of the factors of continuity in my growth, development and learning, no matter what life has presented. The often-used metaphor that comes to mind is the journey of the river. The power of the water is channeled differently as it flows over rocks and through narrows or wide gorges but the flow does not stop until the journey ends in the sea. The river, like passion, finds a way to persist and a means for expression; it pushes the learner to adapt to the contours of the environment in order to reach the final destination—the object of its passion. Interestingly, for my life, I have discovered that while I have objects (or what I have called "components") of desire/passion crop up throughout my life, my deepest passion is not an object. It is not arriving at a destination, but my deepest passion is the actual process—the transformational learning that occurs throughout life.

This river metaphor shows how passion is a dynamic process that is never static. Passion flows through our lives and as it ebbs we need ways of regaining it using such interventions as our Passion Transformation Model. Also, passion may look and feel different at various times in our life. Understanding the process helps us to understand ourselves.

Another one of our interviewees talked about the role of passion for adult learners. She uses the metaphor of an archaeological dig to explain how passion affects adults. This metaphor explains the ever-changing process of finding your passion, as well as the transformation process of "uncovering" the unknown in us. Trudy Candelaria, a speech therapist, said,

> They [adults] recognize that there is worth in the pursuit of the knowledge, that at times there will be difficulties obtaining it, and they realize that they will probably never know the subject in full. I might compare it to an archaeologist at a new dig site. Each turn of the shovel may uncover a myriad of finds just within that square foot. The experienced archaeologist realizes that there are thousands of shovelfuls left to turn and they may never see the sum of all the knowledge there is to know about this site. Yet they keep going—one shovelful at a time—to see what they can discover within the time they have been allotted. The adult learner knows to keep shoveling. They may never uncover all there is to know about their passion, but they will definitely value the dig.

Last, we want to return to the metaphor we have used throughout this book, the fire of passion. Here we look at passion as a process including the spark, the fuel, and the flame.

The Spark of Discovering

Just like a fire needs a match to light it, employees need the spark of Discovering to be set on fire. Many people have told us that they have worked in jobs for days, weeks, years, even decades without questioning their lack of enthusiasm. Sometimes it took an extraordinary event to force them to reevaluate their lives.

The employees in your organization need your help to discover what would make them passionate about becoming actively engaged. The Discovering Process is the spark that helps organizations and individuals find their passion, uncover their problems, barriers, and roadblocks to living, and to be passionate.

The Fuel of Designing

Every fire must have fuel to continue to burn. In your case, the fuel is the environment your leadership team provides employees. Start with yourself. Are you passionate about your work and your company? If not, it will be difficult to inspire others. Find what turns you on and make sure others feel that passion. Second, does your organization have a meaningful and inspiring mission and vision? It's difficult to get excited about an organization that doesn't know where it's going or if it's going nowhere interesting. Many companies have a mission and vision but don't follow them. Make yours a way of life. Third, have you created a supportive, nurturing organization where people feel their work is meaningful, and it is fun to come to work? Are you friendly? Do you support employees when they have troubles, do you celebrate with them when things are going well? Design your organization so that there is plenty of fuel to keep your employee's passion for work burning.

The Flame of Transformation

Once the fuel has been prepared and the spark has been struck, the flame that transforms is lit and sustained. Transformation occurs with risking, learning, and building self-efficacy. Self-efficacy is the belief that you can accomplish what you set out to do.

Every person we have asked has told us that passionate living involves taking risks. Risk-taking leads to learning, which then leads to increased self-efficacy. When employees learn, the belief they have in their ability to perform increases. We've found that when learning slows or stops, so does passion. Give your employees continual challenges, opportunities to learn and try new things, and support them as they succeed or fail. Build reflection, learning, and continuous growth into their jobs and careers.

Conclusion—We Make the Road by Walking

Now it is up to you. It is up to you to create passionate work for yourself or a passionate work environment for your employees. Miles Horton, like many great leaders, did both. Horton was the founder of the famous Highlander Folk School. In starting the school, he said:

The school was started so we could have a place to teach what we believed in. Perhaps a good part of my own personal activities grow out of my desire to be unlimited. I resent anything that hinders the fullest development of my personality or the personalities of anyone else, or any barriers that hinder the fullest development of people anywhere. (quoted in Horton 1989: 27)

You should resent it too. Practice the Passion Transformation Model, seek Occupational Intimacy, and your life will be filled with discovery, continuous creation, risking, learning, and self-efficacy.

Having recommended discovering, designing, and developing your life to reach your goals and creating your organizational environment to be passionate, we also know that things change and people change and it is unwise to stick to plans that are clearly not working. Yes, keep your eye on the goal, but recognize that there are many ways to reach it. There are many paths to any given point on the map; the trick is to find the one that works for you.

Perhaps the best advice is to recognize that the journey itself is what is most important. Designing your future increases the chances of reaching the ultimate goal, increases your personal power, and aligns your life to get what you desire. Looking at it from another perspective, however, we don't live by plans, we live in the moment. During an interview, Paulo Friere, a leading educator and proponent of emancipatory learning, once said, "I think that even though we need to have some outline, I am sure that we make the road by walking" (Horton and Friere 1990: 6).

We do make the road by walking. The path is created as we live each moment, as we make a multitude of decisions that either further our passion or move us away from it. Living passionately in every moment, regardless of circumstance, is what makes life rich.

References

Ackerman, D. *A Natural History of Love*. New York: Vintage Books. 1995.

Alexander, J. *Spirit of the Home: How to Make Your Home a Sanctuary*. London: Thorsons, 1998.

Ambrose, S. E. *Undaunted Courage*. New York: Touchstone, 1996.

Apps, J. W. *Teaching From the Heart*. Malabar, FL: Krieger, 1996.

Argyris, C. *Integrating the Individual and the Organization*. New York: Wiley, 1964.

Argyris, C., and D. A. Schön. *Organizational Learning: A Theory of Action Perspective*. Reading, Mass.: Addison-Wesley, 1978.

Aronson, E. *The Social Animal*, 4th ed. New York: W. H. Freeman and Company, 1984.

Bandura, A. "Self-Efficacy Mechanism in Human Agency." *American Psychologist* 37 (1982): 122–147.

_____. "Human Agency in Social Cognitive Theory." *American Psychologist* 44 (1989): 1175–1184.

Baumeister, R. F., and E. Bratslavsky. "Passion, Intimacy, and Time: Passionate Love as a Function of Change in Intimacy." *Personality and Social Psychology Review* 3, no. 1 (1999): 49–67.

Belenky, M. F., B. M. Clinchy, N. R. Goldberger, and J. M. Tarule. *Women's Ways of Knowing*. New York: Basic Books, 1986.

Bennis, W. "Leaders in Transition." *Executive Excellence* 15 (1998): 5–6.

Blanchard, K., D. Zigarmi, and P. Zigarmi. *Situational Leadership Facilitator Guide*. Blanchard Training and Development, Inc., 1994.

Bleyl, M. "The Wise Ones: A Multi-Cultural Perspective." Ph.D. diss., University of New Mexico, 2000.

Blom, L. A., and L. T. Chaplin. *The Intimate Act of Choreography*. Pittsburgh and London: University of Pittsburgh Press, 1982.

Boldt, L. G. *How to Find the Work You Love*. New York: Penguin Arkana, 1996.

Bolman, L. G., and T. E. Deal. *Leading with Soul: An Uncommon Journey of Spirit*. San Francisco: Jossey-Bass, 1995.

_____. *Reframing Organizations: Artistry, Choice, and Leadership*, 2d ed. San Francisco: Jossey-Bass, 1997.

Boorstin, D. J. *The Discoverers*. New York: Vintage Books, 1985.

Bova, B., and M. Kroth. "Closing the Gap: The Mentoring of Generation X." *MPAEA Journal of Adult Education* (summer 1999): 7–17.

_____. "Workplace Learning and Generation X." *Journal of Workplace Learning* 13, no 2 (March 2001): 57–65.

Boverie, P. "Gender, Motivational Forces, Level of Decision-Making and Risk-Taking: A Phenomenological Study of Risk-Taking in College Students." Ph.D. diss., University of Texas at Austin, 1988.

Boverie, P. E., and M. Kroth. *A Passion for Work: Developing and Maintaining Motivation*. Academy of Human Resource Development Annual Convention Conference Proceedings (March 8–10, 2000): 849–856.

Brehm, S. S. *Intimate Relationships*, 2d ed. New York: McGraw-Hill, 1992.

Branden, N. *The Six Pillars of Self-Esteem*. New York: Bantam, 1994.

Bridges, W. *Transitions: Making Sense of Life's Changes*. Reading, Mass: Addison-Wesley, 1980.

Brookfield, S. D. *The Skillful Teacher*. San Francisco: Jossey-Bass, 1990.

Buber, M. *The Way of Man*. New York: Citadel Press, 1995.

Buechner, F. *Wishful Thinking*. New York: Harper and Row, 1993.

Byrd, R. E. *A Guide to Personal Risk Taking*. New York: AMACOM, 1974.

Cameron, J. *The Artist's Way*. New York: Tarcher/Putnam, 1992.

Campbell, J. *The Power of Myth*. New York: Anchor Books, Doubleday, 1988.

Cather, W. *My Ántonia*. Boston: Houghton Mifflin, 1954.

Chambers, E. G., M. Foulon, H. Handfield-Jones, S. M. Hankin, and E. G. Michaels III. "The War for Talent." *McKinsey Quarterly* 3 (1998): 44–57.

Cochran, L. *The Sense of Vocation: A Study of Career and Life Development*. Albany, N.Y.: State University of New York, 1990.

Coelho, P. *The Alchemist: A Fable About Following Your Dream*. New York: HarperCollins, 1998.

Coles, R. *The Call of Stories: Teaching and the Moral Imagination*. Boston: Houghton Mifflin, 1989.

Collins, J. C., and J. I. Porras. *Built to Last: Successful Habits of Visionary Companies*. New York: HarperBusiness, 1997.

Covey, S. R. *The Seven Habits of Highly Effective People*. New York: Fireside Books, 1989.

Csikszentmihalyi, M. *Flow: The Psychology of Optimal Experience*. New York: HarperPerennial, 1990.

Daloz, L. A. *Effective Teaching and Mentoring: Realizing the Transformational Power of Adult Learning Experiences*. San Francisco: Jossey-Bass, 1986.

Danielou, A., trans. *The Complete Kama Sutra*. Rochester, Vt.: Park Street Press, 1994.

Dominice, P. *Learning from Our Lives: Using Educational Biographies with Adults.* San Francisco: Jossey-Bass, 2000.

Erikson, E. H. *Identity and the Life Cycle.* New York: International Universities Press, 1959.

_____. *Gandhi's Truth.* New York: W. W. Norton, 1969.

Fisher, H. *Anatomy of Love.* New York: Fawcett Columbine, 1992.

Fox, M. *The Reinvention of Work: A New Vision of Livelihood for Our Time.* San Francico: HarperSanFrancisco, 1994.

Frankl, V. F. *Man's Search for Meaning.* New York: Touchstone, 1984.

Freeman, W. C. "Construction of the Psychological Variable Passion and Its Relationship to Productivity in Selected Figures." Psy.D. diss., Adler School of Professional Psychology, 1993.

Freiberg, K., and J. Freiberg. *Nuts! Southwest Airlines' Crazy Recipe for Business and Personal Success.* Austin, Tex.: Bard Press, 1996.

Fried, R. L. *The Passionate Teacher: A Practical Guide.* Boston: Beacon Press, 1995.

Friere, P. *Pedagogy of the Oppressed.* New York: Continuum, 1993.

Gilley, J. W., and A. Maycunich. *Beyond the Learning Organization: Creating a Culture of Continuous Growth and Development Through State-of-the-Art Human Resource Practices.* Cambridge, Mass.: Perseus, 2000.

Gilligan, C. *In a Different Voice: Psychological Theory and Women's Development.* Cambridge, Mass.: Harvard University Press, 1982.

Goleman, D. *Working with Emotional Intelligence.* New York: Bantam Books, 1998.

Gould, R. L. *Transformations.* New York: Simon and Schuster, 1978.

Grantham, C. *The Future of Work: The Promise of the New Digital Work Society.* New York: McGraw-Hill, 2000.

Hamel, G., and C. K. Prahaled. *Competing for the Future.* Boston: Harvard Business School Press, 1994.

Helgeson, S. *The Female Advantage.* New York: Doubleday Currency, 1990.

Herzberg, F. "One More Time: How Do You Motivate Employees?" *Harvard Business Review.* (January-February 1968).

HH Dalai Lama and H. C. Cutler. *The Art of Happiness: A Handbook for Living.* New York: Riverhead Books, 1998.

Hochschild, A. R. *The Managed Heart: Commercialization of Human Feeling.* Berkeley: University of California Press, 1983.

Horton, A. I. *The Highlander Flk School: A History of Its Major Programs, 1932–1961.* Brooklyn, N.Y.: Carson Publishing, 1989.

Horton, M., and P. Friere. *We Make the Road by Walking.* Edited by B. Bell, J. Gaventa, and J. Peters. Philadelphia: Temple University Press, 1990.

Jaffe, D. T., and C. D. Scott. *Take This Job and Love It: How to Change Your Work Without Changing Your Job.* New York: Simon and Schuster, 1988.

Knowles, M. S. *The Adult Learner: A Neglected Species.* Houston, Tex.: Gulf, 1973.

Kogan, N., and M. A. Wallach. "Risk Taking as a Function of the Situation, the Person, and the Group." In *New Directions in Psychology,* vol. 3, edited by G. Mandler,

P. Mussen, N. Kogan, and M. A. Wallach. New York: Holt, Rinehart and Winston, 1967.

Kolb, D. A. *Experiential Learning: Experience as the Source of Learning and Development.* Englewood Cliffs, N.J.: Prentice Hall, 1984.

Kroth, M., and P. Boverie. "Life Mission and Adult Learning." *Adult Education Quarterly* 50, no. 2 (2000): 134–149.

Kuhn, T. S. *The Structure of Scientific Revolutions.* Chicago: University of Chicago Press, 1970.

Leider, R. J., and D. A. Shapiro. *Repacking Your Bags.* San Francisco: Berrett-Koehler, 1995.

Lerner, H. G. *The Dance of Intimacy.* New York: Harper and Row, 1989.

Levinson, D. J. *The Seasons of a Man's Life.* New York: Ballantine Books, 1978.

Lewis, S. *Babbitt.* New York: Penguin Books, 1996.

Lucas, J. R. *The Passionate Organization: Igniting the Fire of Employee Commitment.* New York: AMACON, 1999.

Marquart, M. J. *Building the Learning Organization.* New York: McGraw-Hill, 1996.

Maslow, A. H. *Motivation and Personality.* New York: Harper and Row, 1954.

May, R. *Love and Will.* New York: W. W. Norton, 1969.

McGregor, D. *The Human Side of Enterprise.* New York: McGraw-Hill, 1960.

Mezirow, J. "A Critical Theory of Adult Learning and Education." *Adult Education* 32 (1981): 3–27.

_____. "Transformative Learning as Meaning Becoming Clarified." *Challenges of Practice: Transformative Learning in Action.* New York: Teachers College, Columbia University (2000): 344–346.

_____. "Learning to Think Like an Adult: Core Concepts of Transformation Theory." In *Learning as Transformation: Critical Perspectives on a Theory in Progress* by Mezirow and Associates, 3–34. San Francisco: Jossey-Bass, 2000.

Morris, D. *Intimate Behavior.* New York: Random House, 1971.

Naylor, T. H., W. H. Willimon, and M. R. Naylor. *The Search for Meaning.* Nashville, Tenn.: Abingdon, 1994.

Neel, R. "Take Your Job from Ordinary to Extraordinary." Unpublished workshop. Albuquerque, N.Mex.: University of New Mexico, 2000.

Noer, D. *Healing the Wounds: Overcoming the Trauma of Layoffs and Revitalizing Downsized Organizations.* San Francisco: Jossey-Bass, 1993.

Osborn, A. F. *Applied Imagination: Principles and Procedures of Creative Problem-Solving,* 3d ed. New York: Charles Scribner's Sons, 1963.

O'Toole, J. *Leading Change: The Argument for Values-Based Leadership.* New York: Ballantine Books, 1996.

Palmer, P. *The Courage to Teach.* San Francisco: Jossey-Bass, 1998.

Parks, S. D. *Big Questions, Worthy Dreams.* San Francisco: Jossey-Bass, 2000.

Peck, M. S. *The Road Less Traveled.* New York: Touchstone, 1978.

Peters, T. "Rule #3: Leadership Is Confusing as Hell." *Fast Company* 136 (March 2001).

Peters, T. J., and R. H. Waterman Jr. *In Search of Excellence: Lessons from America's Best-Run Companies.* New York: Harper and Row, 1982.

Peterson, B. *Sister Stories: Taking the Journey Together.* New York: Viking, 1996.

Peterson, C., S. F. Maier, and M. E. P. Seligman. *Learned Helplessness.* New York: Oxford University Press, 1993.

Rapoport, I., and T. S. Wallsten. "Individual Decision-Making Behavior." *Annual Review of Psychology* 23 (1972): 131–176.

Reina, D. S., and M. L. Reina. *Trust and Betrayal in the Workplace: Building Effective Relationships in Your Organization.* San Francisco: Berrett-Koehler Publishers, 1999.

Rilke, R. M. *Letters to a Young Poet.* New York: Vintage Books, 1984.

Rogers, C. R. *On Becoming a Person.* Boston: Houghton Mifflin, 1961.

Schein, E. H. *Organizational Culture and Leadership,* 2d ed. San Francisco: Jossey-Bass, 1992.

Scherer, J. *Work and the Human Spirit.* Spokane, Wash.: Paulsen Center, 1993.

Seligman, M. E. *Learned Optimism: How to Change Your Mind and Your Life.* New York: Pocket Books, 1998.

Senge, P. "Walk into the Future." *Executive Excellence* 16 (1999): 9–10.

Senge, P., A. Kleiner, C. Roberts, R. B. Ross, and B. J. Smith. *The Fifth Discipline Fieldbook: Strategies and Tools for Building a Learning Organization.* New York: Doubleday, 1994.

Sherrill, L. J. *The Struggle of the Soul.* New York: MacMillan, 1951.

Short, J. F., Jr. "The Social Fabric at Risk: Toward the Social Transformation of Risk Analysis." *American Sociological Review* 49 (1984): 711–725.

Simpson, L. *Working from the Heart: A Practical Guide to Loving What You Do for a Living.* London: Vermilion, 1999.

Sinetar, M. *Do What You Love: The Money Will Follow.* New York: Paulist Press, 1987.

Slovic, P. "Assessment of Risk Taking Behavior." *Psychological Bulletin* 61 (1964): 220–233.

Sternberg, R. J. *The Triangle of Love: Intimacy, Passion, Commitment.* New York: Basic Books, 1987.

Suzuki, S. *Zen Mind, Beginner's Mind.* New York: Weatherhill, 1994.

Taylor, E. W. "Analyzing Research on Transformative Learning Theory." In *Learning as Transformation: Critical Perspectives on a Theory in Progress* by Mezirow and Associates, 285–328. San Francisco: Jossey-Bass, 2000.

Tennov, D. *Love and Limerence: The Experience of Being in Love.* New York: Stein and Day, 1979.

Thompson, A. A., Jr., and A. J. Strickland III. *Strategic Management: Concepts and Cases,* 6th ed. Boston: Irwin, 1992.

Tichy, N. M., and S. Sherman. *Control Your Destiny or Someone Else Will: How Jack Welch Is Making General Electric the World's Most Competitive Company.* New York: Currency Doubleday, 1993.

Turkel, S. *Working.* New York: New Press, 1972.

Victoria magazine. "The Business of Bliss." New York: Hearst Books, 1999.

Vroom, V. H. *Work and Motivation.* New York: Wiley, 1964.

Waterman, R. H., Jr. *What America Does Right: Learning from Companies That Put People First.* New York: Norton, 1994.

Watkins, K. E., and V. J. Marsick. *Sculpting the Learning Organization: Lessons in the Art and Science of Systemic Change.* San Francisco: Jossey-Bass, 1993.

Watkins, K. E., V. J. Marsick, L. Honold, and J. O'Neil. "Shaping a Learning Vision: Life Histories of Learning Leaders and Facilitators." *Proceedings of the Academy of Human Resource Development Annual Meeting* (2000): 205–212.

Webster's New Collegiate Dictionary. Springfield, Mass.: G.& C. Merriam Company, 1979.

Weiss, R. S. "The Fund of Sociability." *Transaction* 7 (1969): 36–43.

Whyte, D. *The Heart Aroused.* New York: Currency Doubleday, 1994.

Wilson, L., and H. Wilson. *Play to Win: Choosing Growth Over Fear in Work and Life.* Austin, Tex.: Bard, 1998.

About the Authors

Patricia E. Boverie

Patricia E. Boverie is an Associate Professor and Program Coordinator of Organizational Learning and Instructional Technology in the College of Education at the University of New Mexico. After graduating from the University of Texas in Austin, Patricia taught in the psychology department at Central Washington University, where she codirected a master's program in Organizational Development. She has completed postdoctoral work at the University of British Columbia and Harvard University.

Patricia's areas of expertise are in the fields of individual, team, and organizational learning. She teaches classes in adult learning theory, group processes in learning team development and training, critical thinking, learning to learn, organization development, and consulting theory and practice. In 1996 she received the Outstanding Teacher of the Year Award from the University of New Mexico.

Patricia's research interests include the development of passion in the workplace, evaluation of on-line learning, work team training, and the development of consultant competencies. She has served and is currently serving as an evaluator to Star Schools Project, funded through the U.S. Department of Education. She has published over twenty-five articles and has made more than fifty presentations to international and national associations, including ASTD, AERA, ICED, and AHRD.

In addition to teaching at the university, Patricia is a co-owner of Boverie, Kroth, & Associates, a company that focuses on personal and organizational transformation and the development of passionate work.

Michael Kroth

Michael Kroth has made presentations for local, state, regional, national, and international organizations. His presentation topics have included "Lessons from the Titanic: Finding Personal Purpose and Meaning in Times of Crisis"; "Having the Time of Your Life—The Keys to Effective Time Management"; "Life Mission and Adult Learning"; "The Power of Purpose"; "How to Speak Without (Much) Fear"; "The Call to Teach: I Believe I Can Fly!"; "The Five Foundations for Fulfillment"; "Creating 'Moving' Presentations"; "The Real Phantom Menace: Finding the Force Within"; "The Free Agent Workforce of the Future"; "Mission Impossible: Can Training Transfer Be Assured?"; and "Passionate Work: The Five Keys to Occupational Intimacy."

Michael is a coowner of Boverie, Kroth, & Associates, a company that focuses on personal and organizational transformation and the development of passionate work. He is an adjunct professor at the University of New Mexico in the Organizational Learning and Instructional Technologies program. He recently retired from Public Service Company of New Mexico (PNM) after twenty-two years, during which time he was administrator of the PNM Foundation, Director of Corporate Community Affairs, and a Senior Organizational Consultant.

Michael's focus is on individual and organizational transformational learning processes. He has developed and administered corporate-level leadership development and succession planning programs and conducts a wide range of training and consulting on a regular basis.

Michael is a past member of the American Society for Training and Development's (ASTD) International Conference Program Advisory Committee. In the past he has served as a New Mexico Arts Commissioner, President of the New Mexico Public Relations Society of America, a member of the Goals for Albuquerque Committee, and President of the Albuquerque Arts Alliance.

Index

Printed in the United States
50755LVS00003B/91-108